WHEN CAREGIVERS NEED CARE GIVEN

"Caring For Yourself While Caring For Others"

TWYLIA G. REID

FOREWORD BY OMAR TYREE

WHEN CAREGIVERS NEED CARE GIVEN

Copyright © 2018 by *Twylia G. Reid*. All rights reserved.

Biblical verses are taken from the Good News Translation (GNT) of The Bible

Biblical verses are taken from the New International Version (NIV) of The Bible

Published by BROKEN WINGS
Post Office Box 55
Pooler, GA 31322
www.twyliareid.com

All rights reserved. No part of this book may be reproduced, stored in a retrieval system or transmitted in any form or by any means electronic, mechanical, including photocopying, recording, or by any information storage or retrieval system, without permission in writing from the publisher.

When Caregivers Need Care Given / 1st Print Edition
Twylia G. Reid

ISBN: 978-1-7322063-7-3

Printed in the United States of America

FIRST PAPERBACK EDITION

DEDICATION

I dedicate **"When Caregivers Need Care GIVEN"** first to my Lord and Savior Jesus Christ for giving me the drive and persistence to write yet another book.

Secondly, to the caregivers around the world as a gift of inspiration, encouragement, and motivation to know that we possess the power to indeed move mountains. So, speak life each and every day and watch the changes occur right before your eyes as we continue to grow as we travel this journey together! What do you do when you need care given? My answer is simply this—you do whatever you need to do to make it happen! Live each day remembering you do not have to create a miracle in order to help your loved one have a productive day; it just needs to be predictable. This will allow for a safe and pleasant day for the both of you. Every night before you go to bed, look yourself in the mirror and say these words, *"I am an extraordinary person for having the ability to care for others the way I do, to love others the way I do, and most importantly to love myself in the process."*

Thirdly, to all of the survivors of brain injury and other tragic events, and those who are persevering and handling the challenges that accompanies tragedies.

To my daughter, NaSharee, thanks for being the adult you are even when you want to be the child that you are so entitled to be. I am proud of the woman, mom, wife, and daughter you are. My love for you can never be measured. You make me proud to call you daughter. To my parents, my siblings, extended family and friends, thank you for your encouragement, prayers, and continued support. Whether it was a listening ear, a should to cry on, a phone call to check on Mylon for me when he would not answer my phone call, or a conversation to lift him up when my words just did not seem to be enough, I want to say thank you all and God bless each of you.

To my son, Mylon, our miracle child, as my mother refers to him. Thank you, son, for teaching me what happiness looks like. Each day you get up and get dressed (sometimes several hours before an appointment or work lol) with anticipation of having a good day. You have no idea how much you inspire me to do the same. Although each day is filled with challenges, hurdles, obstacles, and frustrations that only you will ever be able to understand, it gives me joy in seeing you putting forth your best effort to conquer the world no matter what comes your way. As I write this with tears streaming down my face, I want you to know that you are never a burden to me. I promised God on June 18, 2001 that if He allowed you to live, I would do my best to be the best caregiver you would need. Although I make mistakes and do not always get it right, I have kept my word son. I just want you to know that I will continue to pray and believe God for your complete and total healing. Whether it happens on this side or the other side, son, I know you will continue to SOAR by the power of God as you continue making the impossible possible! Remember, in your own words, "We Got This!"

Last, but certainly not least, to anyone affected directly or indirectly by a tragedy of any kind. I understand the emotional and psychological effects that occur after surviving a tragedy have been overlooked far too long. I always say as a caregiver that we are our loved one's biggest cheerleader, their number one fan, and most times their only advocate, so I encourage you to speak to those mountains and command them to move as you care for yourself while caring for others!

Table of Contents

Introduction 17

Chapter 1 Once Upon A Time Long Ago 24

Chapter 2 The Preparation Stage 29

Chapter 3 Oh God, Why Me 34

Chapter 4 When Caregivers Need Care Given 43

Chapter 5 Self-Care 52

Chapter 6 My Defining Moment 58

Chapter 7 My Perspective 63

Chapter 8 My Vision for the Future 69

Chapter 9 Lord Give Me Strength 74

Chapter 10 Fight or Flight 82

Chapter 11 A True Conqueror 87

Chapter 12 Planning Makes Perfect...Or Does It 91

Chapter 13 The New Normal 97

Chapter 14 Practice Gratitude 103

Chapter 15 My Name is Victory 110

Chapter 16 Praising Forward 116

"Caregiver's Affirmation" 123

Scriptures That Speak Life and Keep You Inspired..126

APPOINTMENT REMINDER 132

ABOUT THE AUTHOR 133

ACKNOWLEDGEMENT

Oh wow, where do I start? First, I must say thank you to everyone for their prayers, love, and continued support. There's an old saying that states, "It takes a village to raise a child." Well, I can honestly say it takes a village to support an author! I have been beyond blessed to have been truly supported by a village of phenomenal people.

Yet again, there is no way I could have made it this far as a caregiver without God. I always say He puts something special on the inside of caregivers that allows us to care for our loved ones in a special kind of way. I know, without a doubt, I could not endure this journey without His comforting loving arms each day. Thank you God for choosing me to be the "one" to nurture, protect, and love on Mylon until he is safe in your arms in Heaven. To my husband, Dexter Reid, who for some strange reason hangs in here with me on this rollercoaster of a journey called caregiving. And, oh what a journey it is! The silent frustrations you deal with are not silent at all; they are actually deafening to my ears. Although you are not as active in the actual hands on caregiving piece as I am, your existence brings a sense of ceasefire in our home that is often needed during the times I need them the most. I guess it is safe to say you are the caregiver of the caregiver who not only gives care to Mylon, but to others as well. I am convinced God knew what I would need along this journey and that is why He sent you to find me. Thank you, my love, for being the husband and father in our lives you have been. Thanks for not quitting and giving up. Many may not understand this, but they don't have to. Just know that I love you now, will love you tomorrow, and forever. To my daughter, NaSharee Davenport, thank you for being there when no one else is. Thank you for the breaks you give me even when I know your agenda is full and you really don't have the time or energy to do so. Being a big sister has been a role you have taken to an entirely new level. I know God was intentional when He gave you to me. Mylon is blessed to have you as his big sister, and I am honored to call you daughter.

To my parents, Arthur and Vera Flournoy, thank you for praying for me and being there. I love you both more than you can ever imagine. Vonka, Kevin, and I are blessed to have you as our parents. You both are the epitome of what right looks like. The wisdom and knowledge you both have poured into us have shaped us into the adults we are today.

To all my extended family, friends, and fellow writers, too many to mention by name, I am grateful and thankful for you all. Some have been here with me from the very beginning, and some I have been blessed to meet along the way. They listened with caring ears, gave me shoulders to cry on, and helped keep my spirit positive.

I want to give a wholehearted thank you to Brittany Gibbs who didn't hesitate when I told her I needed someone to edit the book. Here willingness and kind heartedness enabled me to move forward with ease. I also must thank every single person who purchased a copy of *Broken Wings* and helped catapult me to where I am today. Your prayers, support, text messages, emails, and phone calls mean more to me than any of you will ever know. The love you all have shown me has been immeasurable and I truly thank God for each of you.

FOREWORD

A Woman's Nature

By Omar Tyree

Amazingly, I just had a stirring conversation and group discussion on a podcast radio program on Monday night, October 22, 2018, all about entrepreneurship and taskmasters, who are able to cut friends, family and associates off and push them back to get your work done, no matter what. I explained that I had the tough-love gene for separation early on in life, going all the way back to my teenager years, when my friends and family already knew that I had no time to get bogged down or to wrestle with any of them when I needed to do what I needed to do.

At that time, my important duties included my homework assignments, football practice, saving my money, arriving at the movies on time, and making whatever decisions I needed to make about my personal goals on my own and without a whole lot of conflicting influence from others.

All of the roadblocks of family, friends and associates can create a much slower path to your personal goals of success, as well as cripple your decision-making process that stops you from moving forward in a timely fashion on things that you know you need to accomplish.

The professional women on this podcast interview went on to highlight the ability to "cut others loose" in order to get things done as some sort of extreme struggle, but I looked at it all as a necessity of a focused life. I've been cutting folks back for nearly fifty years to get things done, to the point where they didn't even complain about it. My people simply called me "focused" on what I needed to do, and that's why I was able to get so much accomplished, including the writing and publishing more than twenty-five books.

However, as our radio discussion continued, one of the professional women on the line made note that "cutting loose" was much harder to do for women, because their natural instincts and desire to nurture others and make sure that everyone is well and satisfied, often made them feel guilty about stepping away or moving on. I was then forced to reflect back to my boss-lady mother—the oldest in her family of eight—and my generous maternal grandmother, who took different family members into her crowded home every single week, including my paternal grandmother who seemed to raise all of her grandchildren, as if they had no mothers or fathers. I then thought about my own wife, and how she often complains about doing everything for everyone else and nothing for herself.

I often argue, "Well, stop doing it then." But it's not

that easy. Caring is a woman's nature, it's her natural DNA.

Now, please don't go overboard with this idea of naturally caring women, because there are definitely thousands of rogue women out there who just don't give a damn. Nevertheless, I would look at them all as the exceptions to the worldwide rule.

Therefore, author Twylia Reid's book, *What Do You Do...When Caregivers Need Care Given*, immediately struck me as a woman's book. Not to say that men cannot be professional or family caregivers, but it's definitely not as natural of a task for us men as it is for women, who've been raising and caring for nations of people in the absence of men for thousands of years. Those are the facts.

So this book becomes an important read and resource not only for professional caregivers at home, in hospitals, nursing facilities, homeless shelters, daycare centers and so, but for caring mothers, sisters, aunts, grandmothers, teachers and men like myself, who need to *learn* more about the stress and strain of those who are far more attached to the welfare, needs and desires of others than what I've ever been.

We all need to be educated not only how to care more, but how to respect, understand, honor and help those who spend their whole lives caring for others, because caring is a *must* for all of us.

Just imagine a newborn baby in this world of able-minded and bodied adults not having anyone to care about their milk, a change of diapers, burping, a comfortable place to sleep, silence, and the basic human interaction that every child needs to develop, survive and grow into normal, functioning and productive adults?

None of us would ever survive without caregivers. Even the mythology of *Tarzan* and the *Jungle Book* had loving animals who became the needed caregivers to help these mythological characters to survive and grow into functional humans.

In the case of Twylia Reid and her son, the consistency, courage, frustration loneliness and ultimate success of their incredible story for more than twenty years of love and care will continue to be inspirational for everyone who reads and knows it, which qualifies Sister Reid as a veteran in the field of understanding the compassion, sensitivity, motivation and willpower needed to maintain as a successful caregiver.

What Do You Do...When Caregivers Need Care Given is a must read!

~ **Omar Tyree** is a ***New York Times*** bestselling and **NAACP Image Award** winning author of more than twenty-five titles in various genres and subjects.

Introduction

Being a caregiver can be a difficult role. It requires patience, sensitivity, selflessness, and hard work. Providing care for someone, whether it's a child, a parent, a loved one, or as a professional necessitates a high level of self-love and self-care. Caregiving can feel rewarding and hard at the same time. But while it may be a rewarding experience to care for a loved one, the emotional and physical stress of caregiving far too often leads to burnout and exhaustion, causing caregivers to put themselves and their own well-being in the background.

Caregivers often feel stressed, neglected, and oh yea...very alone. So, what if the person in need is the caregiver themselves? What do you do when the caregiver needs care given? How can you fulfill your role as a caregiver without losing yourself?

After an individual sustains a debilitating injury of some kind, family members are thrown into a whirlwind of various emotions and decisions about their loved one's care. Grief or a sense of loss may be associated with the uncertainty of the situation and changes in the survivor. Spouses, partners, parents, siblings and children may suddenly experience role changes associated with becoming a caregiver for their loved one. As such, they may experience an increased responsibility for providing physical, financial and emotional support at a level they are not used to providing.

Feelings of hopelessness and helplessness became my daily dose of what I felt my life was going to be. I had no clue how much my life was about to change. Not just my life, but all those connected to me as well. You see, being thrusted into an unwelcoming situation and unforeseen circumstances was a journey I did not think I was going to be able to handle. All of my Christian beliefs somehow seemed to vanish and for the life of me, I just could not conjure up the lessons of faith I had heard and been taught throughout my life.

What was I to do? I will tell you, I truly had to dig deep and trust that God was truly going to make a way out of no way. After all, that is what my grandmother used to say all the time. Well grandma, I can truly say that now I know exactly what you meant!

So, who is a caregiver? To be honest, most of us at some point in our lives have been a caregiver. Caregivers are people just like you and I. They are daughters, wives, husbands, sons, grandchildren, nieces, nephews, parents, and friends. While some people obtain care from paid caregivers, most are forced to depend on unpaid care and support from families and friends. Some live in the same house with their loved one, and some live far away. Some may be full-time or part-time. Believe it or not, some caregivers even care for other family members while caring for their disabled loved one as well.

A caregiver's responsibilities can include a number of things, from house cleaning, to cooking and bathing, to managing doctor appointments or finances, to being a best friend, a counselor, and so much more. Some caregivers even have a more hands on role if their loved one needs assistance getting dressed or going to the bathroom.

No matter how much love is between a caregiver and their loved one, caregiving is NOT an easy job, and it gets harder as those you care for get older. Being a caregiver takes a toll on your job, your family's lives, and most of all your personal life. Almost all caregivers at some point may experience anxiety or irritability stemming from their roles, because it is a very demanding job.

I have listed the major types of caregivers to whom many organizations refer. Just as myself, many of you may even fall into more than one of these categories:

- Primary Caregiver – This term applies to someone, normally a family member, who takes on the role of caring for their loved one while receiving no financial reimbursement. They are the backbone of the person they are providing care for. They are sometimes referred to as family caregivers. They provide emotional, financial, nursing, social, home-making, and other services on a daily basis for their loved one. Their job is a 24 hour a day job which may include duties such as: personal care, cooking, feeding, toileting, dressing, bathing, carrying out routine medical procedures, giving medication, and managing a household. Primary caregivers experience the highest levels of fatigue and caregiver burnout. They often operate in this role while taking care of other family members as well. In regards to family law, a primary caregiver is normally the parent who has the greatest responsibility for the daily care and rearing of a child. In some cases, this person may be a nonparent.

- The Crisis Caregiver – This applies if your loved one is efficient and functional, and does fine on his or her own until an emergency situation arises that calls for you to then step in. Oftentimes, crisis caregivers may not live in the same home as the person they are providing care to; however, they may live nearby. This can be a parent of a child with special needs who may have a roommate. The child and parent reside in the same city and state in near proximity of one another.

- The Working Caregiver – This applies if you are working a part-time or full-time job in addition to taking on the caregiving role of providing care for a loved one. The working caregiver may often experience caregiver burnout, especially if they have a family they are responsible for taking care of as well. More than 1 in 6 Americans working full-time or part-time report assisting with the care of an elderly or disabled family member, relative, or friend. Caregivers working at least 15 hours per week indicated that this assistance significantly affected their work life. [Gallup-Healthways. (2011). Gallup-Healthways Well-Being Index.] Many working caregivers may risk the loss of their income if they have to reduce their work hours or leave their jobs because of the level of care their loved one may require. This in turn could cause them to lose employer based medical benefits. If this occurs, money saved becomes limited due to having to pay caregiving expenses.

- The Sandwich Caregiver – This term applies to adult children who have the responsibility of not only taking care of their own children and family, but their elderly parents as well. The term "sandwich" means they are sandwiched between two generations. Sandwich caregivers also often experience a high level of caregiver fatigue and burnout. Taking care of multiple loved ones at once can bring joy and satisfaction as long as you are taking care of yourself too. These caregivers have a lot on their plates which can lead to high stress levels and priorities that fall by the wayside, especially those who inherit this role overnight.

- The Long-Distance Caregiver – This term applies to a caregiver who lives in a different city, state, or even country but provide care to a loved one. They are normally responsible for the financial, medical, and personal needs of their loved one and provide assistance via telephone. Most family caregivers who are long distant caregivers live at least an hour away from their loved one. Although they live in a different location, many have the same concerns and stresses local caregivers have. Actually, most have more because they normally have to spend more of their own money on things like hiring help for their loved one due to not physically being there, or taking time off work and traveling when he or she needs to come and see about them. However, the most substantial task that the long-distance caregiver faces is staying informed and assured their loved one is in good hands when they are not around.

My prayer is that this book will become a companion for you as you face whatever challenges, trials and tribulations that cross your path as you travel on this caregiving journey. Just remember one thing, you are not alone, even though you will have days when you feel that you are. I also pray that if my own children ever find themselves bearing the role of a caregiver, that they too will find something of value in the pages of this book.

This book is a true story from my own experience, and I hope you will find the content relatable, yet understanding that I am no expert but a mom who has traveled this path since 2001, and has done all I can to ensure that my son's quality of life is meaningful in spite of the challenges he faces as a severe traumatic brain injury survivor.

The most important lesson I have learned as a caregiver is that it is a powerful life changing facilitator for individual growth. The one thing I can promise you is that you will be a different person at the end of it all. You will look at life through different sets of eyes. You will no longer take for granted the things in life you thought would always be there; like being able to dress yourself or feed yourself. With that being said, I sincerely wish you all the best as you travel this caregiving journey and beyond.

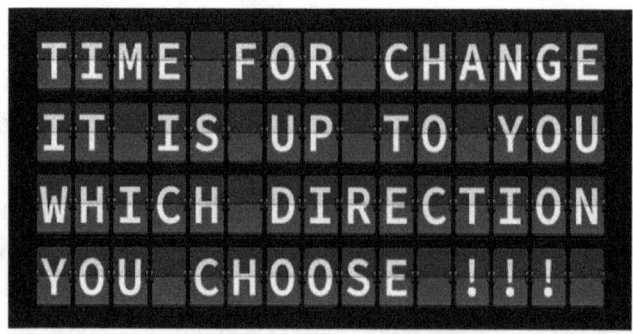

Chapter 1
Once Upon A Time Long Ago

Life for me growing up was filled with love, hate, happiness, and sadness. My parents worked a lot and my siblings and I spent lots of time at our grandparents' house. Childhood was fun and full of games, hot summer days, and nights filled with family love. Eating dinner, sitting around watching television, and enjoying time with my brother and sister was the life! I was the oldest so making them ask mom for ice cream after dinner was just the thing to do since I knew she would tell them yes. I did not have a care in the world, just happy-go-lucky, bill free, and worry free!

My father worked at a factory in our town, and my mother was a telephone operator. Wow, a telephone operator. Do they even have those anymore? I do not think so. Anyway, my siblings and I had a pretty decent life. We really never wanted for much and my parents made sure we had the best of whatever there was to have back then.

Saturday mornings were oh so heavenly—waking up to the smell of salmon croquettes, fresh biscuits and rice topped off with the sweet aroma of tea cakes filled my grandparents' house. Eating breakfast and watching cartoons was a ritual that was never broken. To this day I still find myself enjoying a big bowl of cereal as I watch a cartoon on a calm quiet Saturday morning whenever I can, which trust me, is not quite often. Sitting in the swing on the front porch or on the couch on the back porch, with the huge fan that cooled the entire house is where I often wondered why I felt I was a tad bit different from my siblings and cousins. No one really knew but I use to feel that my life was going to be different from theirs somehow.

Sunday was church time! Going to my grandmother's country church was the best experience ever. The preaching, the music, the praising and shouting are all memories that I will never forget. Why? Well, because during those times I was taught about the goodness of God and how He sent His only son Jesus to come and die on a cross for our sins. True, there were many things I did not understand until I became an adult, but those memories will be forever embedded in my soul. I even remember the day (Wednesday) I got *religion*, as they called it back then! Ha, ha... As I think about that night it makes me chuckle because during the summer revival I actually did feel something that I had never felt before. It really was like fire burning in my bones. Uhm... maybe that particular feeling has stuck with me all these years for me to mention it at this very moment. Who knows? All I know is that it was a feeling that I had never felt before and I liked it. No, actually I loved it! Although I did not really understand what getting saved truly meant, one thing I did know at that young age was that if being saved meant feeling God like this, I wanted it! Little did I know, this was the beginning of my journey of experiencing God, and all His marvelous splendor.

The summer months were absolutely the best. My cousins and I would play outside at my grandmother's house until the street lights came on. That was our sign that it was time to come in for the evening. Walking to the neighborhood park to watch the baseball games or walking barefoot to the YMCA for an afternoon swim with my baby sister as we complained due to the heat from the asphalt burning the bottoms of our feet are priceless memories. That was the life I tell you, and nothing or no one could ever tell me that life would be anything other than this. I had my life all planned out. I would marry my prince charming, maybe have a kid or two, have a fabulous career and live a very calm and peaceful life! I have always loved the water so I vowed I would live near the ocean. I always loved being outside so I also vowed I would live in a place that always had nice weather. God's creation has always been fascinating and phenomenal to me. I was always in awe of just how spectacular He is, even though I may not have understood it all back then. I shared this to demonstrate how the simplicities of life can mean the world to you and should never be taken for granted. I shared it to paint the picture of how important it is to always live in the moment and appreciate the goodness of it. The Bible clearly instructs us to only worry about today. Now I understand why.

Although I had life all planned out, little did I know what life had in store for me. Nothing, and I mean absolutely nothing, in this world could have prepared me for what I was to endure, or so I thought.

Now, let us fast forward to my college years.

NOTES

Chapter 2
The Preparation Stage

College was my preparation stage to caregiving. My roommate was a really sweet girl we got along really well. She was witty and very intelligent; however, she was in a bad relationship. I always felt like it was my duty to be there for her, to talk to, to mentor, and to be a shoulder for her to cry on. I always made sure we had food in our pantry and that we had the essentials we needed to live off of. I never expected anything in return from her. I never got angry when she would spend her money and buy things for him and not purchase items she needed. All I knew is that I was there for her for a reason, and that she needed me. We would sit and talk for hours about life, as we knew it, as well as the things we desired in life for each of our futures. I always felt like her counselor. I was not much older than she was but yet I felt as though I had been in this world before. I cannot recall the number of times we laughed and cried together. No matter how many times I told myself that she would be ok, I just could not stop playing the role of big sister to her.

She always informed me of where she was, what she

was doing, and who she was with. I would always remind her to call her parents at least twice a week to check in with them. I do not know if it was because of her controlling boyfriend or what, but I always worried about her and wanted the best for her. Nights when she would stay out with him I would worry about her and pray that she was okay. I would not feel at ease until I would see her face the next morning; it was really like a sense of relief to me just knowing she was ok.

After my freshman year in college I moved back home to attend the local college in my home town. The feeling in the pit of my stomach grew deeper each day as my last day on campus approached. The thought of what was going to happen to my best friend, my roommate, my confidant plagued me. I would pray each day and ask God to watch over her. I even secretly prayed that her boyfriend would suddenly have to leave the school and never ever return. Yea, I know it was cruel but hey it is the truth.

The day finally came for us to say our goodbyes. I gave her a necklace with a cross on it, and we vowed to always keep in touch with one another. The both of us cried because somehow we knew we would never see each other again. And you know what, we never have. I wonder whatever happened to her...

Well, after college, and years of working, I decided to go into the military. This is where the real preparation began. God had a plan for me, but I was too blind to see it. Although I had grown up in the church and heard about how test and trials come to make you strong, I really did not think too much about that. No matter what job titled I held or performed, I also had others I was responsible for providing caring for. Whether it was to just sit and listen, or actually do something to make the person's life a bit easier, I was always the one. God was always putting people in my path that needed assistance of some kind. I would spend countless hours doing research, several days cooking food, months of caring for the needs of others. That's just who I was and there was nothing I could do to change it.

During my time in the military, from day one, I always had Soldiers that were involved in some sort of dilemma. Some had come from broken homes that just needed nurturing and a sense that someone could actually care for and love them. Some were involved in really bad relationships, verbal as well as physical. Some had never been away from home and just needed a mother figure for guidance and wisdom. Whatever the need was, God had equipped me to fulfill it. No matter what it was, I was there. *Momma Sergeant* is what my Soldiers called me. And, it was really funny because regardless of where I was stationed in the world, I played the same role! It was really weird but I enjoyed how God was using me to witness to and minister to whomever He placed in my path. Once while stationed in Korea, I remember my husband and I cooked Thanksgiving dinner for about eight of my Soldiers. They were unable to go home so we decided to ensure they felt the love of family and had enough food to take home and last them for a few days. This was just one of the many ways we took care of them and made sure their parents knew they were in good hands. Many even gave their lives to Christ and attended church where we worshipped. And guess what? Almost every Soldier I had still stays in contact with me. A lot of them are now wives, husbands, moms or dads and I am very proud of them all. One day I remember asking God what He was up to and why, because it was during these times I begin to quickly realize the things occurring in my life indicated He was indeed up to something. I recall the conversation like it was yesterday. I said, "God, I don't know what you are doing, and why you are doing this but whatever it is can you please not let it not be too painful for me to handle". The routine had become all too familiar so I knew He had to be preparing me for something, and that something was going to be BIG!

NOTES

Chapter 3
Oh God, Why Me

Well, June 18, 2001 God decided to reveal to me what He had been preparing me for. This was the day my life was changed forever. It was the day God decided to reveal to me just what He had in store for my future. It was this day I had no choice other than to fight or flight. My son and I were involved in the worst car accident ever. Being hit by three vehicles as we were traveling home, literally three blocks from where we lived, left a permanent stain that has not been erased. One of the vehicles actually entered into my vehicle upon impact and struck my son directly. His lifeless limp body laid slumped over in the back seat as I desperately tried to open the car door to no avail. Climbing over the seat to get to him was all I cared about. As I held his blood covered body in my arms, I cried out to God for help like never before. "God, please don't take my son from me!" I was numb, helpless, and in shock. I could see what appeared to be hundreds of bystanders as I yelled out in utter desperation. As my cries grew faint, I could feel my heart beating out of my chest. The lump in my throat was so huge that I could not breathe because it was cutting off my air flow. The sweat from my face mixed with the blood streaming from my head trickled down my face. As they met my tears, they dripped on me and my son as I cradled him in my arms praying like I had never prayed before. At that moment, God had mercy on me and He heard my cry. A young man opened my car door and said these words to me, "I'm a doctor, and I am here to work on your son." A feeling of relief rushed over me and I knew God had showed up on the scene! A lot took place at that moment that I will never forget. A lady appeared out of nowhere and assisted me. She wrapped my head with the top I had on and gently led me away from my car. Her touch was soft, her voice was soothing, and she smelled like roses. I remember breathing in her scent as she stood over me trying to clean the blood from my face. The sweet fragrance of rose petals seemed to put me in a trance as it over powered the smell of the blood which kept streaming down from underneath the shirt she had wrapped my head with. Upon arriving to the hospital, people were scurrying around in a frantic. Doctors, nurses, and people seemed to be everywhere. I was able to make a phone call with one of the nurse's cell phone. I called my family to tell them what had occurred. I really could not talk because I was still numb from all that had taken place. All I could do was scream out Mylon's name to my sister on the other end of the phone. The nurse had informed my family a little bit of what had just occurred. I remember my sister and mother on the phone, but whatever words they said to me is still a blank. You see, I had literally blacked out emotionally and mentally. I did not know the extent of what had happened nor did I really understand just how critical and serious the accident we were involved in really was. The surgeon who operated on my son had come in to try to get my consent to operate on him, but I did not really understand all she was saying because as stated previously, I had emotionally tapped out. The one thing I do remember is her eyes being red as an apple because she had been crying. That should have alerted me of the seriousness of my son's injuries, but hey, I was so far gone I did not realize that even I had sustained several broken ribs. Well, to sum this all up, after his surgery she returned and leaned over the stretcher I was laying on and said to me, "He made it out of the surgery, but he's not out of the woods yet. He's sustained a severe traumatic brain injury, and right now is in a coma on life support." The next breath I took seemed like my last. It was long and deep and I let out a sigh of relief just knowing he was still alive. Little did I know, this was just the beginning of a life filled with twists, turns, and various challenges that would take me on the ride of my life—a life filled with ups, downs, highs, lows, and most of all, loneliness and isolation. Not just for me and my baby boy, but my daughter as well. Life as we all once knew it was no more. Being thrust into bleak circumstances and uncertain outcomes into a world of the unknown was the least of what we experienced on this day.

Still not being able to understand, this is what God had been preparing me for. I was not coherent enough to actually see it. It had not registered just yet that all of the training God had taken me through was for this very moment. The thoughts in my mind were far from realizing that I was indeed prepared to deal with this. All I knew was my son was lying there in front of me on life support, and nothing or no one really mattered at that time.

I recall one day sitting on the floor in the hallway of the Pediatric Intensive Care Unit thinking to myself. So many questions, so much doubt, so much anger and rage, so little faith had consumed me. "How was I going to be able to do this?" is what I kept thinking to myself. I did not know whether I was going or coming. I was literally a nervous wreck! Filled with fear and confusion, my days and nights were filled with lumps in my throat and butterflies in my stomach. I just wanted to curl up on that floor and die. Yeah, that was it. I thought if I was no longer here then I would not have to deal with all of this. At that moment, I felt like the worst mother in the world for even thinking such a thing. I cried uncontrollably and asked God to please forgive me and to give me the strength I needed and was going to require to face the biggest challenge of my life.

I had no idea that the caregiving life was going to be this way. I had several days of not knowing how to plan what needed to be done. This in turn caused me to have headaches and anxiety which stopped me in my tracks. After finally putting a plan in place, I found myself having to go back and redo it all over again, and again, and again. This became my norm. My life had dissolved and I had developed into a walking minute-by-minute scheduler and planner. Watching my son go through rehabilitation was difficult. Nonetheless, I made sure that I was present for each and every one of his sessions. I watched attentively as the therapist worked with him, learning every move, each technique, and strategy they used. I mastered them all and even added a few things of my own. "Besides, who knows what works best for my son other than me," I always thought. I kept boxes and boxes of medical records, doctors and nurses' notes, whatever I thought I would need to be the best caregiver I could be. There was one horrible incident that occurred while he was in inpatient therapy that really PISSED ME OFF! Mylon had completed his morning and afternoon sessions for the day. He still had his feeding tube in so the nurses had to come in and pour his liquid lunch, as I called it, into his feeding tube. He must have been really tired this day because after his dinner, he fell fast asleep. So, I thought this would be the perfect time for me to go across the street to the local department store and purchase a few items I needed for myself. I was literally living in the hospital with him. I had a cot that sat in a corner of his room which I slept on each night. For some reason I just wasn't able to leave the hospital. I was so afraid to even go home and get a change of clothes. I went to the nurses' station and informed them that he was asleep and that I was going across the street for a few minutes. They assured me they would keep an eye on him and not to worry. One nurse even told me, "You need a break. You've been in this hospital since day one." Well to say the least I nodded, said thank you, and proceeded to the elevator. I peeped into the room and my son was still asleep. When I arrived at the department store I just kept feeling like something was not quite right. I kind of dismissed it and thought to myself that I was overreacting, but the feeling just would not go away. I cut my time in the department store short, paid for my items, and hurried back to the hospital. When I arrived back on the floor, the nurses where still sitting at their station working quietly. I immediately felt that I was just panicking for nothing and that all was well until I walked into my son's room. What I saw made me furious! My son was sitting up in his bed, which zipped from the outside, covered in feces! I screamed and the nurses came running into our room. The look on their faces was a look of terror. But, the look on my face was the look of rage! "How could you all allow this to happen?" I asked. "I asked you all to look after him while I go across the street!" I yelled. All along I was thinking to myself, "I have done so much for my son since he's been here. I change his bed, change his clothes, bathe him, clean the room, and all they have to do is give him his liquid lunch and administer his medication." Those things I could not do simply because I was not a "nurse". The more I thought about it, the angrier I became. I demanded they leave immediately and boy did I mean it! They exited the room quickly to retrieve clean linen to change his bedding. I changed my clothes as fast as I could, put on flip fops and unzipped his bed. I helped him out his bed and put him in his wheelchair and rolled him into the bathroom. I quickly undressed him, placed him in his shower chair, and wheeled him into the shower. Drenched in water, I bathed my son that evening and made a vow to him from that moment on that he would never have to worry about anything or anyone overlooking him, mishandling him, or mistreating him ever again. Tears rolled down my face as I kneeled down on my knees to clean his feet. The slight stream of tears became a sob and before I know it, we both were weeping uncontrollably. After cleaning him up, and drying him off he felt much better. But, I was still in wet clothes. With water dripping from my hair I looked like a wet rag doll. He looked at me and grinned. I dressed him in nice warm pajamas, put lotion on him and brushed his hair. I had to be very careful because he had an indention in his head from where his skull was still missing. He wore a bicycle helmet every day and only took it off to shower and at bedtime. As I looked at him, I knew in my heart he knew that he was safe and all was well. I pushed him out of the bathroom and got him safely in bed. We said our prayers and he turned over and closed his eyes. As I watched him fall asleep, I prayed and asked God to watch over us both that night. I went into the bathroom and looked in the mirror and starred at the woman looking back at me. The person I saw was not the person who came into that hospital on June 18, 2001. Her hair was thinning in the area glass had been embedded in her scalp, bags were underneath both her eyes, and as they welled up with tears, I simply looked up towards heaven and asked, "Oh God, why me?"

I did not understand why God would allow this to happen. I thought I was a good person; one who loved Him with all my heart, and soul. I just could not understand why this was happening. I did not understand why my heart was aching the way it was and why my son and I were going through this ordeal. All I knew was that this was a pain I had never felt before and it was a feeling I did not like. The tears I had shed were countless. I stopped keeping count of the number of days I had awakened with tear drenched pillows or the number of times I had said to myself, "This too shall pass." I stopped because I was simply drained, frustrated, and confused. My heart ached as I was watching my son literally fight for his life. And me, of course, fighting along with him, and praying that he continued to have the strength to do so…day after day, no matter how long it took.

By the way, I never told you the answer I got from God when I asked Him "Why me?". Well, it was really quite simple, He merely replied "Why NOT you." This was that eye-opening moment when the replay of all of the training, tests, and trials I had endured were finally revealed! "Oh, WOW God!" I shouted. "So, this is it uh? This is what you have been preparing me for?" Even though I got the answer to my question, I still was not ready! I still felt in my heart that nothing could have prepared me for what was to come.

NOTES

Chapter 4
When Caregivers Need Care Given

Days passed as seconds turned to minutes, minutes turned to hours, hours turned to days, days turned to weeks, weeks turned to months, and yep you guessed it, those months have now turned into years. Am I depressed? Wait, me? What is this thing I have been feeling lately? I spend significantly more hours per week providing care, dealing with personal stress, battling mental and physical health problems, experiencing lack of sleep, finding less time to do the things I enjoy, and definitely spending less time with my husband, other family members or friends. My daily challenges make it harder for me to get rest or assistance in providing care. Uhm, am I really depressed? Maybe I am.

Caregiving can continue for years. Research has shown that long-term caregivers are at higher risks for depression, burnout, and medical issues because the mind and body are always connected and are in constant communication. Every day there are complicated interactions between our thoughts, emotions, body, and the world around us. Gee whiz! It is an ongoing battle that seems to never stop until one day, it actually does.

If you paid me a million dollars, I still could not tell you how many times I have shed silent tears. Days filled with so much frustration, heartache, and pain to the point of almost no return. Nights filled with loneliness, despair, and thoughts of, "What if I could just end it all." Uncontrollable tears that just would not stop despite how hard I tried or how fast I wiped them away that kept coming and coming…and coming. A pain so deep that no matter how many times I pulled up my big girl panties to face life head on, the challenges would just not go away.

As I watch the tears roll from my son's eyes and down his face day after day; I feel the pain in his heart. The look on his face always gives room for letdown which seems to make the gaping hole in my soul bigger every time I look at him. I take note of how he wants to give up and quit no matter how much I try to encourage him to keep going. There are no words or actions to let go of and dismiss the reality of being lost in an unfamiliar place every second, minute, day, month, and year. Long, relentless battles of being isolated inside yourself while others around you never having a clue as to what you are dealing with are often his daily realisms. His constant companion is also my son's greatest adversary – Traumatic Brain Injury.

I am his primary caregiver and each day as I step into his world of confusion and bewilderment, I often question my own sanity as I ride the chaotic, hectic, and unruly waves of his invisible disability. Several times a day I grab my head, close my eyes, and scream silently to myself, "I just don't know what to do anymore." I keep my tears silent and hidden, so I can be readily available to wipe away my son's. Yes, my silent tears collected on pillow cases, tissues, and in some cases, my shirt sleeve are in an enormous cave of pinned up emotion as I struggle through each day. I struggle through the countless moments when my heart breaks into a thousand pieces as I watch the fragments of his life unravelling into a million pieces. Days and nights filled with headaches, fatigue, heartburn, sore feet, and even fluctuation of weight loss and gain, I often ask myself, "My GOD, am I truly built for this?"

Depressive disorders can make you feel exhausted, helpless, and hopeless. Such negative thoughts and feelings can make you feel like giving up. It is important to realize that these negative views are part of the depression and may not truthfully reveal the situation. Below are guidelines adapted from the National Institute of Mental

Health offering recommendations for dealing with depression. [i]

- Set realistic goals. (This is key to do so in light of depression as you may not be able to complete as much as you are adapted to when you are not feeling well.)

- Break large tasks into small ones, set some priorities, and do what you can as you can.

- Try to be with other people and to confide in someone you know and trust; it is often better than suffering alone.

- Participate in activities that may make you feel better, such as exercise, going to the movies, going to the mall, or attending a religious, social, or community event.

- Expect your mood to improve gradually, not immediately. Feeling better takes time. It won't happen overnight.

- It is wise to delay in making important decisions until the depression has lifted. Before deciding to make a major transition—change jobs, get married or divorced—discuss it with others who know you well and can offer another view of your situation. Your view may be distorted due to the depression causing you to think unclearly.

- People rarely wake up and are no longer depressed. Those who expect you to do this are misguided in their understanding of your condition. Remember, they are looking from the outside in and may not really know what you are dealing with.

- Positive thinking and the practice of new surviving patterns will replace the negative thinking that is part of the depression. The negative thinking will be reduced and lessened as your depression responds to treatment.

Say yes to offers of help and commitment by family and friends who you know and trust. They really want to see you get better, so let those who are willing help you along the way. When times like these occur do not be afraid, ashamed, or feel guilty if you need to call upon support in providing care for your loved one. Agencies that provide services such as respite care relief are great and come in handy when you just want to get away. Listen up, there will be many times when you will need to just get away. Positive feedback from others, and positive self-talk and fun occasions are always great self-care practices. Look for classes and support groups available through caregiver support organizations to help you learn or practice effective problem-solving and coping strategies needed for caregiving. Being able to simply talk to others who truly understand what we go through is golden. For your health and the health of your love one as well as others around you, take some time to care for yourself. Not only will you thank yourself for doing so, but those around you will be happy you did.

I learned some time ago about mobile mourning. I did not realize this is what I was actually doing until I learned about it. This term is used to describe the prolonged grieving process experienced by survivors of someone who has experienced a traumatic and life-changing injury. Most commonly, people discuss mobile mourning within the context of traumatic brain injuries. This is because brain injuries can be very stressful for family members and loved ones of the people who are injured. I learned very early as a caregiver to a brain injury survivor that the devastating effects of a brain injury not only affect the survivor, but they reach out and touch all those attached to the survivor as well. A growing tribute of the stress and grief associated with the frequent vague and uncertain diagnoses related with such injuries has led to greater support for people who may experience mobile mourning. This is why it is so important that we take care of ourselves, although I realize this can be an overwhelming task to accomplish, especially when others in the family are working and you are the sole caregiver. However, you must never forget how stress harms the body, especially the immune system, and not to mention how it speeds up the aging process, shortens the life span, and can create an atmosphere that promotes disease.

Caregiver syndrome or caregiver stress is real. It is a condition that strongly manifests exhaustion, anger, rage, or guilt resulting from relentless and constant care for a chronically ill loved one. Although it is not listed in the Diagnostic and Statistical Manual of Mental Disorders, the term is often used by many healthcare professionals around the world. For me, it is often the simplest things I do that make a huge difference in how I manage my caregiving. I realized those with severe cognitive and behavioral changes, as my son has, have no control over their lives. So, giving them choices when challenging moments arise can create a more cooperative spirit. In our world, it is always easier for me to change the environment or atmosphere than to try and change him.

Patience, understanding, more patience and more understanding are the main ingredients in everything I do. The feelings of resentment and sadness over the loss of my son I knew and loved before his brain injury are normal. For a very long time I did not use to think so, but now I know differently. It was not always easy learning to love this new and different son God had given me but with time, strength, determination, and staying power, I realized my work and commitment to optimism was indeed helping him be the best survivor that he can be. FAITH plays a vital role in the quality of life for him and I. It will do the same for you and your loved one as well. Try to develop strategies to manage the things you cannot control, and find a peaceful middle ground to the things you can control. Life for you and everyone else will just become a bit sweeter if you do.

I must say, my son is a fighter. Through the daily pain and challenges, he gets up each morning to live his best life over and over again. Sometimes I feel as though he is my caregiver. His smile is infectious and no matter what kind of day I am having, it keeps me going. It teaches me that despite what I face or what each day brings as his caregiver, tragic events do not have to keep us captive causing us to live in lack, or in a deep pit of depression.

The tears are still there, however. Crying has now become a survival technique for me. Having a good cry can sometimes be just what the doctor ordered. In fact, some psychologists even suggest that we may be doing ourselves harm by not crying on a regularly basis since it is believed that crying may actually be connected to the body's natural healing systems. Crying releases stress, and is therefore a great practice when it comes to staying mentally healthy, especially after dealing with the devastation that accompanies a tragic event. I guess I can move on from this part now.

Just remember if you can find safe spaces to cry in your day-to-day environment, do it! Go ahead and cry, scream, let it all out because it will become easier for you to reap the physical and emotional rewards of crying without fear of anyone seeing you, hearing you, and most importantly without guilt or shame.

NOTES

Chapter 5
Self-Care

Most of us who are caregivers did not choose the role that we now find ourselves in— I know I did not! Normally, it is a title imparted upon us by an unimaginable and untimely occurrence. For me, I found that I was ill-prepared, uneducated, and so unaware and uninformed of what it would involve. I knew absolutely nothing about traumatic brain injury and was not ready for the devastation this monster would bring.

Millions of caregivers are generally providing care for a family member. Research shows that we are at a greater risk for emotional, mental and physical health issues due to the level of responsibility we acquire. Yet, so many caregivers, like myself, continue to do so anyway. It just became second nature, a part of who I am, it is in my DNA, and it is who God has called me to be.

Self-care is important, but some people think it is selfish or inconsiderate. As a matter of fact, I use to think that way about myself. I never really took the time to take care of myself. Here is another truth moment.... sometimes I still do not. Although I do more now than I use to, it is still not enough. I use to feel that if I left my son's side that some God-awful calamity could happen and I would never be able to forgive myself. Talk about CAREGIVER BURN OUT! I was exhausted to the tenth power, daily! It was not until I started to see physical manifestations of my own health deteriorating that I realized I was actually dabbling in self-harm. Yes, self-harm because my lack of self-care was literally killing me softly. Avoiding the things that made me physically and mentally well stole my confidence and self-esteem. I lacked a relationship with the most important person in my life... ME.

As I have stated throughout the book, caregiving is a stressful environment. Feelings of frustration, anger, helplessness and hopelessness are not uncommon when a family member is ill. Those feelings are magnified to much higher levels when you are actually the one personally responsible for the sick or disabled family member. God forbid if it is your child or your parent. There is nothing you will not do to ensure they have all they need or want. As a caregiver, it became second nature to put my son's needs above my own. However, doing so increased my risk of physical disorders such as headaches and joint pain, weakened immune systems, infection and slower healing times.

So, when the chronic migraines began to occur two to three times a week, my stomach began to be upset several times a week, the weight packed on and would not leave, and the aches and pains were just too much to bear, I knew I had to do something different and something drastic. Self-care is important for your mind, body, and soul — your overall health. Without self-care, your relationships with others can suffer immensely. For me fatigue took over. I was not able to spend time with my husband, family members, nor friends like I really wanted and needed to. All I wanted to do was lay around when I did not have to ensure if my son or others around me were being taken care of.

It had become too much, I was slowly slipping away. Although I looked happy and content on the outside, I was miserable, lonely, and wasting away on the inside. So, I decided the best way to truly practice self-care was for me to implement minor, but important, self-care habits daily. I researched both the importance of inner and outer self-care. The information I discovered opened my eyes and helped me understand if I was not taking care of myself, there was no way possible I could be taking care of my son the way I should be or needed to. I came to terms with myself at that moment and made a conscious decision to do better about making sure I incorporated self-care habits into my daily routine.

My goal for this was to maintain a level of optimal health for myself. The World Health Organization says: "Health is a state of complete physical, mental and social well-being and not merely the absence of disease or infirmity." Now, although I absolutely love this definition, realistically, it can be hard for some people to obtain "complete physical, mental and social well-being" with myself being one of those people. Not saying we all should not try to strive for this, but, *realistically* uhmm.... yea, you get where I am coming from. For me, optimal health is personal. It is something an individual must decide to achieve depending on where they have been, and where they are now in their own personal lives health wise.

As a caregiver, optimal health is about being as healthy as only you can be. It has nothing to do with anyone else but you. The ball is always in your court, so if you want optimal health, you need to eat nutritiously and move your body regularly in ways that are appropriate for *your* fitness level. I started looking back over the years accessing my self-care habits. I began to realize how years of poor nutrition, and lack of activity were choices which had now caused me to feel the consequences of these bad decisions. The excess pounds which had accumulated on my body, the increased stressors I had allowed to creep in, and the lack of sleep were all contributing to the kind of slow, steady damage to my body that sets the stage for disease. I had to choose to make changes that would make me feel better every day so that I could continue protecting my future health, as well as that of my son.

Keeping active while caregiving, is one way to help you stay grounded and grateful. Nevertheless, I understand this is probably the last thing on your mind as you tackle the daily challenges of caregiving, but it is something you must find time to do. Exercise for caregivers is vital because it helps to reduce stress hormones, such as cortisol, in the body. In exchange, the body increases its production of endorphins. We all know endorphins are our natural, feel-good chemicals that occur in the body. When endorphins are released, through exercise, you will experience a boost in your mood. As a 17-year caregiver, I need all the mood boosting I can get, which is why I try to walk at least three days a week. You may not believe this, but even the smallest changes to your routine can make a big impact on your overall well-being. Simple adjustments such as parking further from the door when you have to go out shopping, or taking the stairs instead of the elevator, add up over time.

One thing I found to be really cool, was finding things I could do with my son which allowed us both to gain the benefits of these adjustments. I do advise you to check with your primary doctor before starting any new activity, but definitely do so because it is an opportunity for you both to enjoy doing something fun. Walking, light stretches, seated exercises, or other light outdoor activities are all things that you and the person you are caring for can enjoy together. Like the song writer says, "I like to move it, move it!" The important thing is to move and keep moving!

NOTES

Chapter 6
My Defining Moment

What do I mean by my defining moment? Well, I am glad you asked. You see, I had to take some time to really evaluate what had taken place. I had to assess what it meant to me personally. Why did I think this was happening? I could not allow my family and friends to tell me why they think things had happened, I literally had to dig inside myself and do a *gut check*, as I call it. You know, a self-assessment and say, "What does all this really mean to me?". Then, I had to apply some optimistic meaning to it all. It had to be something meaningful, and bright, even though it was the worst thing I had ever experienced in my life.

I know you are probably thinking that this is really difficult to do, especially if it is something really catastrophic, but it is necessary in order to get through it. If not, going through a tragic event can literally take you out, physically, emotionally, and mentally.

I had to do it to maintain my sanity. Hence, I must admit, although this was one of the worst things I had endured; it was only one of many for me. I know in hardships and tragedies it is hard to believe that anything good can ever come from it but one thing I did know and one thing I can say is that it has made me stronger. Going through the heartache and helplessness helped me realize I was stronger than I had ever imagined. I had to be for us both. My son's life, as well as my own was depended upon it. I became wiser and more knowledgeable, and guess what, so will you.

Recognizing the defining moments in your life will enable you to improve and refine your best talents to help you live purposeful, fruitful lives. Doing so helped me discover the necessary actions needed to create the positive, critical turning points in both my son's and my life to keep us afloat each day. This is when I truly began to draw motivation and inspiration.

Say that you determine the defining moment of what you went through was to teach you something. Maybe it occurred to give you a new challenge to do something. Maybe it was for you to see you need to love more, or to forgive more. Or, maybe it was for you to see you need to have more compassion, understanding or patience. Whatever it is, the important thing is that you get it. I had to look at myself and really take an inventory of the things I thought I was doing that was pleasing to God, but really was only doing for myself. Now, I am not saying that tragic events happen to teach us a lesson because we are lacking in some areas. What I am saying is make sure you take the time to do a self-assessment and learn something in the process of it all.

If you can do so, that is AMAZING! It demonstrates your ability to recognize there was indeed something in the tragedy to teach you something to give you a positive outlook on life. And, guess what, that is the beginning of your healing right there. Once you are able to do that, you have got to hold on to it for dear life and never let go. Holding on to it will help you be able to look at things and say yes, this tragedy did happen, yes it was a negative experience, yes it was devastating, yes it was horrific. You will even be able to say yes it was heart wrenching, heartbreaking, and overwhelming, BUT some day, some way, and somehow, I will be strong enough to be able to help someone else make it through.

You must remember there is hope, and where there is a will there is a way. Trouble does not last always, and weeping may endure for a night but joy will indeed come in the morning. Our journey is living proof that joy will come in the morning. I am living proof that even when *caregivers need care given*, that happiness can and will come in the morning.

You see my defining moment helped me to realize that a traumatic even does not have to be the end, and no matter what it looked like with my physical eyes, I had to stay strong and begin to look through my spiritual eyes to see the beauty that was to come in the end. Pinpointing this life changing moment of my journey allowed me to make the most of my potential, discover my own passion, and become the best caregiver I can be. I had to say to myself that I had the power to make a decision, and I had the power to make a choice. I could react to the tragedy that took place as a fearful, negative, bitter, and hurt individual or choose to convert that energy and negative feelings and emotions into a positive reality.

Will it be easy? NOPE, of course not. Will it be sudden? Who knows? Maybe for some, but it was not for me. Oh, but boy when it did, the vision God gave me to go forward with has been empowering, transformational, and life changing. So much so, I now am able to educate and enlighten others to help them create lifelong changes and see the glass half full instead of half empty. I now see the light at the end of this journey. I now understand my purpose and see my *why*, and know without a shadow of a doubt it is to ensure God's name is glorified through it all!

NOTES

Chapter 7
My Perspective

Perspective is the way a person sees the world. It comes from their personal point of view and is shaped by their individual life experiences, values, their current state of mind, the expectations they bring into a situation, and many other things. There is a reason we were taught the saying, "This too shall pass". We have all heard that. Well, this is our reminder of PERSPECTIVE. What...? Yes, perspective. So, there you have it, your great revelation of the day. It is a reminder to us to say, "Hey I know this tragedy looks bad, and is hard to deal with. I know things aren't looking good right now, but in due time things will get better. Sooner or later it will hurt less. Sooner or later it will change and the pain will subside. Sooner or later the heartache will become easier to bear." It will improve over a period of time. This too shall pass—PERSPECTIVE!

I know there are incidents where some tragedies leave everlasting outcomes such as chronic ailments, internal illnesses, or even paralysis. Based on these diagnoses, the person affected knows he or she may never fully recover, but that does not mean you have to be held captive in your mind. This does not mean you have to live in deficiency and in minimalistic circumstances having your quality of life taken away. Your hopes and dreams do not have to be swept away or pushed aside. You can have a positive outlook. You can always improve your heart, mind, and spirit. You must also keep perspective of yourself as well.

What I am saying is that you must never forget how you were before you became a caregiver. Before the tragedy occurred, you demonstrated strength, vitality, agility and courage. Although you may have struggled through it, you made it through all of the challenges you faced. If you are reading this, then guess what? You are here NOW, you are ok NOW, and you are the same person you were before the tragedy. You can always be like me and say, "Hey, every cloud has a silver lining." You think I say this because I am a hopeless optimist and do not know what else to say? No, I actually say it because most times I am right. ☺

Although that silver lining cannot, and will not ever make up for the tragedy, and maybe it is not something that makes you feel vindicated and justified in the struggles you have experienced, but it will allow you to hold on to the hope of things getting better and easier with the dawning of each new day. Fortunately, that silver lining is perspective.

Some people learn perspective at a very early age, and others when they are considered to be over the hill. Nonetheless, once they obtain perspective, whether through tragedy, regret, or something else awful, they realize how important it is, and wonder how they lived without it. I did and so can you. What I realized about perspective is that it did not make my problems go away. It did not fix the tragedy I endured, nor the struggles, challenges, or the regret. It did not take away the pain and unbearable heartache I felt. However, it did allow me to make the decision to live the rest of my life, from the moment I truly gained perspective forward. It reminded me of what was actually important, like the fact that I should take the time to be kind to people because you never know what they are going through, or how much time they have left. It reminded me that life is short and you can be here today and gone today. It reminded me that I should not spend hours worrying over something that should have been decided in a matter of minutes.

Perspective establishes clarity and brings order to issues for you. Wow, how cool is that? It allows you to unquestionably see which problems are big and which are not; what you really need to be concerned about and what can wait. Frustration and defeat can easily creep in when others around you are not able to see things clearly, but perspective allows you to help them when chaos seems to be setting in. In the middle of what can seem like the biggest tragedy you have ever experienced, perspective can save you, and keep you sane. It can be something you gain when it seems as though all else is lost. It can be comfort when you need it the most, peace in the midst of your storms, and the handkerchief that dries the tears others never see you shed.

Think about this, have you ever felt like the car you

were sitting in at a stop sign or traffic light was rolling backwards? When in fact your vehicle was actually sitting still and not moving at all, but the vehicle next to you was moving forward. What occurred was that you automatically and instinctively judged your own movement based on something that was not really happening, but on what your mind believed was happening. Every now and then what we see, experience, and believe is not completely real. It is sort of like a visual effect, a magic trick if you will, where what the physical eye sees is not true. It can be difficult to gain proper perspective at times. Even so, real perspective helps you to gain a better understanding of the truthfulness and accuracy of your experience.

As caregivers, we are constantly struggling to understand the world around us and to find happiness and meaning in each of our lives. We do indeed see things that are not really as they seem. The challenges that accompany tragedies can become too many to keep up with. Although most of them are life-altering, they are not life- summonsing. Ultimately, there is only one thing you can control in life. It is the only thing that no one else in your world can change or correct in any way, regardless of the circumstances or situation. And that my dear friend is *your* perspective. Every one of us has the capability to decide whether we want to view the struggles and challenges that essentially guide our *"caregiving life"* as a task or job to be endured and completed, or as a kind of opportunity to learn from, progress and experience. Once you begin to accept that your perspective can be only controlled by yourself, you will begin to experience life differently. You will decide what to keep and what to throw away. Your day to day journey will become one of self-empowerment, where you are able to decide to what degree you will struggle with or accept the challenges, tests, and trials of life.

To fight alongside your loved one and make a conscious decision to live compassionately and caringly with them as you both maneuver throughout each day traveling this survivor/caregiving journey gives life an exceptional outlook and meaning. It allows us to open our eyes wide and see we are here to be the example of what right looks like - to be the kind of caregiver to not only assist the one we are caring for, but to also help one another so we can experience the full scale of what life truly has to offer. With a positive and optimistic perspective, we can experience gratitude for simply waking up in the morning and realizing how blessed we are to be here to see a new day filled with God's grace and mercy, just as I did as a child. This will replace any feelings of sadness, anger, guilt, and anxiety of you being able to make it through each day while keeping in mind that every cloud really does have a silver lining!

NOTES

Chapter 8
My Vision for the Future

Having a vision for the future keeps and has kept me grounded and enthused. It motivates me to persevere and move forward. It is your responsibility to make yourself see positive things to keep pressing forward towards that thing that you see as your positive. Remember, everything in life starts with a vision. For me, having a vision and implementing that vision was definitely a lot harder than it seemed. Having the vision was only half of me getting there. The other half was the execution of my vision, but even before that came the planning phase. You see, I see my son as the bright, intelligent, vibrant young man he was destined to be. I see the fight in him to succeed despite the challenges he faces from his brain injury. I see the determination in him to never give up no matter how many times he fails. I see him as God sees him. This is what gives me the motivation to keep on keeping on being the best caregiver, mom, servant, wife, and Nana I can be. Basically, the best at whatever I need to be. I had to learn how to define my vision through writing it down to the smallest detail. I had to write it down until I could not describe it anymore, and even then, I had to write some more!

To sum it up, I had to write the vision and make it plain! The word grounded is used in various ways. There is a certain stability connected with being grounded, for the word specifies a firm footing, or rootedness. When we are grounded, we are able to dream big, desire more and work hard towards our dreams, while appreciating the work it takes to achieve these dreams. Being grounded helps me see the cup half full instead of half empty, because I know that with Christ I can indeed do all things because He gives me the strength to do so.

Most of you probably have a general idea about what you want for your life. I know obtaining the role as a caregiver has changed this in many ways, however, you still should have some idea. Having a clear and exciting vision for the future and the ability to communicate that vision has been vital for me staying grounded and inspired. Effective caregivers take the time to think through and develop a clear picture of how life will look in one, three and five-year increments. They make sure to start small. Setting two or three goals at a time and doing all you can to achieve these is the key. Once you adapt this practice of goal setting you too will find achieving your goals easier to do.

Motivating the one you are providing care for to give their best is critical to both of you all's survival. It is my vision of future possibilities of what can be for my son that stimulates and awaken emotions and motivates him to give his best. And when he gives his best, it stirs up my will to keep giving mine as his caregiver.

Practicing patience under pressure is also important when it comes to keeping a vision of the future. Keeping your cool in a crisis means to practice patience and self-control under difficult or disappointing circumstances. Believe me, there will be many difficult and disappointing times you will encounter.

Your vision of the future must stay on the front lines as you navigate through this maze as a caregiver. Your vision is a mental picture of the result you want to achieve. Your vision cannot be an uncertain desire, dream, or hope. It must always be a picture of the real results of real efforts. This is important because it comes from the future and advises and rejuvenates the present. Keeping a vision of the future has become the most powerful tool I have used in surviving this journey as a caregiver. I do not know what I would do or where I would be if I did not keep a vision. Learning the power of my words helps me to visualize this future for my son and I. Constantly speaking life into the beginning of each day commands it to be all that God intends for the day to be for us.

Your vision is powerful because it inspires action. Powerful visions attract ideas, people and resources that are needed to help maintain a healthy atmosphere. It creates the liveliness and will also make change happen. It will inspire you as the caregiver and your loved one to commit, endure, and give life your very best. Each day I get up, I reflect on my vision for the future. I keep it simple, yet detailed enough for me to see, smell, and taste it. You must do the same down to the smallest details. As the caregiver, you must do all you can to stay positive. Being positive takes me to places I never knew existed. It allows me to meet people I never thought I could. Sure, you have permission to acknowledge the difficulties, but do not try to motivate yourself or your loved one with a vision of bad things that might happen if neither of you succeed. Fear-based visions for the future may help generate unexpected action, but it can also limit your results to damage control rather than getting to positive change.

Last, but certainly not least, allow your vision to come from your heart and not your head, self-help books, or advice from family and friends. Do not try to think your way to a vision. Trust me, that method does not work. Creating a vision for the future that will be exciting and engaging should be your goal. This allows my son and I to frequently participate in activities together which produces fond memories that I tuck away for future moments when I may need them the most. So, in order to do this, you must give yourself the freedom needed to dream and use your imagination to see and feel all the things you want to happen in your life for you as well as your loved one that does not yet exist. You are your biggest advocate! I say this more than I realize because it is the absolute truth. Not just for your loved one, but for yourself as well. Always remember to guard the matters of your heart for in it holds the visions for your future as a caregiver.

NOTES

Chapter 9
Lord Give Me Strength

Inner strength is just as important as outer strength for caregivers. Being able to tolerate the day to day emotional, mental and physical challenges I deal with oftentimes become unbearable, intolerable, and yep even sometimes agonizing. As caregivers we possess much strength— more than we realize we have. Are you aware of your individual caregiver strengths? What about your internal resource? You know, the Holy Spirit? Sometimes do you just stop and ask yourself what your greatest strength is as a caregiver. This is definitely something to make you go uhm....

One of the consequences of surviving trauma is that I started to see danger everywhere. Suddenly, everything had the possibility to kill me, or harm me and my children. It became hard to shift my mind away from all the worst-case scenarios waiting behind every corner. My own streak of neurotic obsessive thinking, which I am willfully continuously working on, is dwelling on these dangers and wondering when and how I will meet the next major tragedy in my life. My doctors call it Post Traumatic Stress Disorder (PTSD).

But here's the thing: I try to remember that I cannot control it all. Indeed, it is very important for you to be able to recognize your caregiver strengths and then pull from them to shape and form your caregiving. As a caregiver, I sometimes feel overwhelmed and swamped by the constant stresses of the caregiving role and caregiver responsibilities. My days and nights often run into each other causing me to feel helpless and hopeless. By focusing on my strengths and know-hows I bring to this role, I am able to take greater control over my experiences, causing me to feel more capable as I improve my overall well-being. It helps me maintain my sanity I tell you, while ultimately leading me to become a happier person. You will as well as you begin to practice the same technique. I began struggling to understand my son, and realized most times he was also struggling to understand me as his caregiver. We were both finding it difficult to comprehend and appreciate why the other did the things we did. As stated earlier, as the caregiver, it is best to always try to look at the positive in all situations. The best we can do is to allow ourselves an extra breath to ask, "What's really important at this moment?" Then, let go, let be, and let GOD do the rest.

So, I ask again, "What are your caregiver strengths?" Determining your own strengths may actually be difficult at first, as it was for me, because I had been only focusing on my son— the person I had been caring for and not my own self. Coming to terms with my caregiver strengths is what I had needed to do for quite some time. It was just the thing that gave me the push to realize just how powerful I am as a caregiver. Once you take a deep breath and begin to realize your caregiver strengths, it will do you and the person you are caring for a world of good. Once you recognize the inner resources you already have, you can then develop an action plan to apply these resources to counterbalance difficulties and challenges you face as a caregiver.

Just think about your personal strengths. These are strengths we are born with. God created each of us in His image, therefore we possess strength that is like no other. We possess the power to move mountains with just faith the size of a mustard seed, which by the way, is as small as a pencil dot. This is the strength that has brought us caregivers this far. It is the strength that helps us get up each morning to face another day in spite of the tears and heartache. It is the strength that allows us to look in the mirror and smile knowing that everyday can indeed be a good day. Yea, that strength that is your personal strength. It is the internal quality that helps us deal with the challenges of life as we travel this journey. When you can discover that strength, you may very well discover other hidden caregiver strengths you never knew you possessed. Now, would that be just grand! Yes, I thought so as well when I discovered mine.

When it comes to these caregiving strengths, I simply ask God to help me with these things:

1. **Resilience** – The ability to withstand or recover quickly from difficult conditions; I can negotiate for what I need and navigate systems.

2. **Patience** – The capacity to accept or tolerate delay, trouble, or suffering without getting angry or upset.

3. **Flexibility** - Ready and able to change so as to adapt to different circumstances; accept what is happening in the moment.

4. **Compassion** - The ability to translate empathic feelings into action (desire to alleviate suffering).

5. **Optimism** – Expect a favorable or positive outcome.

6. **Confidence** – Sure of one's self and one's abilities.

7. **Organization** - Methodical and efficient in arrangement or function.

8. **Perseverance** - Steadfastness in doing something despite difficulty or delay in achieving success.

9. **Ability to Laugh** – To easily see and appreciate the humor in the situation.

To identify and recognize your personal caregiver strengths, you will need to set aside a few minutes each day to conduct personal assessments. This is not hard to do. Simply ask yourself these questions:

- What gives me spirit and energy?
- What am I good at and do best?
- What comes naturally to me?

- What are my best personality qualities?
- How do I handle challenges when I faced with them?

When doing this, you do not have to worry about self-judgement or ridicule. Self-judgment is how you view yourself mostly in a critical way. It is normally due to a lack of self-belief, and usually occurs whenever one starts to compare what he has done to what he thinks he should have been done or to what someone else has done. It can also occur when those around you offer their two, three, or maybe even more cents as to how you should have handled a particular situation.

I love doing this personal assessment and I do it as often as I need to. I never worry about having to go back and examine my answers so I can answer from my heart. They are for my eyes only. So, as you do your very own self-assessment, just remember it is for you and you only. This is a time for you to be honest with yourself on what you do really well, and/or not so well. You may find out that you are well at certain activities, or that you have a certain character trait. You may find out that you handle stress a lot better than you realized. You may even discover that you are capable of handling all of these very well. Or, you may also realize you need help in some areas. IF this is the case, it is ok. I REPEAT, if this is the case, it is ok! You will find your way, soon and very soon. This assessment is wonderful. It allows me to evaluate and assess myself. I am able to measure what I know, what I do not know, and it even helps me figure out things I want and need to know. It helps me in recognizing my own strengths and weaknesses right before my very own eyes!

Below is another exercise I find helpful and do frequently as well. You can do this to help you concentrate on those strengths you just asked God to help you with as a caregiver. Your job is to decide the strength of your agreement with each statement, using the following scale:

    1. All the time 2. Sometimes 3. Hardly ever

I see myself as someone who is...

1. **Resilient** (All the Time, Sometimes, or Hardly Ever)

2. ***Patient***

3. ***Flexible***

4. ***Compassionate***

5. ***Optimistic***

6. ***Confident***

7. ***Organized***

8. ***Able to persevere***

9. ***Able to laugh easily***

Now that you have identified, acknowledged, and written down your personal caregiver strengths, you can become the best caregiver you can be! You can strategize and formulate a plan by joining the strengths together you are well at and applying them to your daily experiences and activities.

Developing an actual caregiver's action plan may not be a bad idea. I had to. Once I actually realized the areas I was strong in, as well as the areas I was not so strong in, I was able to put a plan of action in place which consisted of a regular routine, a daily schedule, which by the way included some me time, emergency rosters, and some other useful tools. My life changed for the better and became much more manageable. Using what you have learned to help you manage your daily challenges can help your life become much easier to deal with as well, and much more productive for you and the one you are caring for. ☺

NOTES

Chapter 10
Fight or Flight

Fight, flight or freeze, are normally the three responses we show when we are faced with dangerous or overwhelming situations. Wikipedia defines fight-or-flight response as "a physiological reaction that occurs in response to a perceived harmful event, attack, or threat to survival."[ii] [The fight-or-flight response refers to a specific natural chemical reaction that we experience during intense stress or fear. The sympathetic nervous system releases hormones that cause changes to occur throughout the body. It is simply the body's response to seeing something that can be a threat to us or cause us harm. During this reaction, certain hormones like adrenaline and cortisol are released, speeding the heart rate, slowing digestion, shifting blood flow to major muscle groups, and changing various other autonomic nervous functions, giving the body a burst of energy and strength.

As a caregiver my stress levels often keep me on a high fight-or-flight alert. Fortunately, there is now an option that has been added to these and that is to challenge.

The challenge response causes you to look at your stress as excitement, which in turn helps you to actually perform better.

I can see how this can be an added benefit. Several instances have occurred when I had been faced with overwhelming challenges regarding my son that forced me to either look at the situation and totally freak out or try to give him cues to divert his attention to something else by trying to make him laugh or make the situation a happier one. Effective caregiving strategies involve of all of the things we do for ourselves that we know work well when we are involved with caregiving. It is almost like you do what works when it works and not worry about anything else at that given moment. I know how exhausting it can be. Oh God, trust me I know! But, I have learned to ask myself, "What works?" I was determined not to fall into the trap of many caregivers: doing what I saw other caregivers do and feeling like, *"Hey if it works for them, it must work for me"*. I had to always keep in mind that caregiving also points back to ourselves, therefore realizing that what works for Tierra may not work for Leah. Or, what works for Jeremiah may not work for Dezmond. I have to simply keep my eyes open at all times and do what works for my son and I at that particular time.

When I finally came to terms with the fact that stress produces real physical changes in the body, I knew I had to activate the tools and strategies I had absorbed. In some unknown way, the fears in my mind, both conscious and unconscious, were causing my hormones and immune system to act in ways I was not used to. Oh no, this caregiving life had started to alter my physical body! What was I going to do? Why was this happening? Who was going to give me the care I needed? What was going to happen now that I, the caregiver, needed care given!

Dr. Janice Kiecolt-Glaser, along with her team of researchers at Ohio State University Medical Center, has found a chemical marker in the blood that shows a significant increase under chronic stress and is linked to an impaired immune system response in aging adults. One of their studies found that caregivers had a 63% higher death rate than the control group they had put together. About 70% of the caregivers they were studying died before the end of the study and had to be replaced by new subjects. Another surprising result was that high levels of IL-6, an immune system mediator protein, continued even three years after the caregiving stopped. Dr. Glaser proposes the prolonged stress may have triggered a permanent abnormality of the immune system.

So, what can we do? Well, there are some things we can do to ensure we are taking care of ourselves. Take time off when you can. Taking a break from caregiving is just as important as taking a break at work or taking that vacation you have been talking about for five years or more. Go ahead, plan a weekend trip or get-a-way, and make arrangements with family members or friends to give you a break from caregiving. Ask people that you trust so not only will you have a stress-free break but so can the person you are caring for.

There are also resources available like assistive technology to help assure that your loved one is taken care of in case you need to leave for brief moments. Equipment like emergency alert bracelets, pendants, and GPS tracking can also be used if your loved one is inclined to wandering off. Other items such as remote video surveillance with your in-home security system, sensory amplification, and other variants of assistive devices are available to help disabled people manage on their own.

Next, try your best to remove as much stress that is not related to caregiving as possible from your home, job, and other surroundings. It does not take rocket science to figure out if you can remove other stressors in your life that are unnecessary, especially those that are added by outside people, places, or things that only bring added chaos. Doing this allowed me opportunities to better deal with the stressors of caregiving, which I did not want to or could not remove.

Attending workshops to help learn about different techniques and strategies to do this are normally available. Some are personal workshops or virtual ones. These workshops will become learning experiences and opportunities for you to find help with your own caregiving situation. Support groups, mentoring programs, and programs offered by state agencies can offer valuable coping strategies as well. Learning that you can create the life you desire in spite of the challenges you face is your goal. It is one that you can and will achieve if you stick to it!

NOTES

Chapter 11
A True Conqueror

According to Merriam-Webster's Dictionary, "one who conquers: one who wins a country in war, subdues or subjugates a people, or overcomes an adversary."[iii] An adversary is looked at as someone or something that is an enemy or opponent. June 18, 2018 made 17 years that I have been dealing with my worst adversary, my most challenging opponent. Who or what is my opponent, you may ask? My son's traumatic brain injury—the ultimate adversary! Why? Because it is of the unknown. It can affect all facets of an individual's life, including physical ability, communication, and mental health, and present chronic health conditions that persist throughout their lifespan.

Watching my son battle with brain fatigue day in and day out as he combats with this opponent is heart wrenching. It is very difficult and tiring for his brain to think, process, and organize, stop, and do it all over again. Crowds, confusion, and loud noises quickly overload his brain, because it does not filter sounds as well as it used to. Limiting and regulating his exposure is a coping strategy, not a behavioral problem. If there is more than one person talking, he may seem uninterested, unconcerned, and disengaged in what they are saying. That is because he has trouble following all the different parts of the discussion. It is draining for him to keep trying to piece it all together, and keep up with what everyone is saying. He is not dumb nor rude; his brain is getting overloaded. He does not want you to know because he does not want to risk the ridicule and judgement, so he retreats to a place within himself. So, what you get is isolation, separation, and sometimes harsh words, but if you just take the time to look deep into his eyes, you will see that he is still there crying out for your understanding and patience.

As his mom and caregiver, I try to get others to evaluate the present circumstance if a conduct problem arises. *Behavior problems*, as many may call it, are often an indication or signal of his inability to handle or actually cope with a specific situation, and not a mental health issue. He may be frustrated, in pain, overtired or there may be too much confusion or noise for his brain to filter.

I advocate for him by educating others to understand that patience is the best gift you can give him because it allows him to work purposely and at his own pace, allowing him to reestablish the lanes in his brain. Rushing and multi-tasking never work; they only delay and deter cognition. Please listen to me with understanding, and listen to him with patience. Try not to interrupt. Allow him to find his words and follow his thoughts. I have to remind others that this helps him to rebuild his language skills. To be honest, sometimes I have to remind myself as well.

You may be wondering why did I just share all of this with you? Well, I want you to see that he is the real hero here. He is the true conqueror and the reason I do what I do. Although the progression of recovery following his traumatic brain injury has been long and demanding for us both, neither of us give up. The process of the person you are caring for will vary and fluctuate. However, we the caregiver normally progress through several phases of recovery which include disbelief, grief, and most of all, difficulty with acceptance. When thinking about the future for us both, I experienced a grieving process that included redefining me, fear of long-term caregiver stress, and reevaluating my expectations.

As a result of providing the bulk of care for my son, I've experienced changes in my physical and psychological well-being. The impact of changes was due to the level of injury he had sustained as well as the progress or lack of progress over time. Research has found that caregivers may experience greater distress than the person they care for, and symptoms of anxiety and depression can impact a caregiver years after their loved one's injury.

NOTES

Chapter 12
Planning Makes Perfect...
Or Does It

Some people take on the role of caregiving without giving much thought to it. That is how it happened for me. All I knew and saw was my son in need, so without hesitation, my nurturing instinct kicked in and never stopped. Rarely do I stop to think about the responsibilities caregiving really involves, or that it is a role I could be taking on for years and years...and years to come.

Becoming an effective caregiver, especially to someone with a life-long debilitating illness means that you must have a plan in place. Having a plan helps me with the unexpected changes that occur. Without having a plan in place, you leave the door open for a plethora of things to go wrong. God forbid if those unexpected changes were to occur with your loved one's health. Without the correct legal and financial documentation, you and your loved one could be faced with issues beyond your control. Here are a few examples: doctors may refuse to discuss important medical information with you, which could affect your loved one's quality of life in a major way; their bank accounts, property, and personal belongings could be passed on to people they do not know if they become incapacitated. Hence, why it is imperative and vital to have a plan.

Likewise, you as the caregiver can help your loved one plan for their current and future medical and financial needs by helping them prepare the following legal documents: medical documents to include a HIPPA Authorization, Heath Care POA, and a Living Will or Advance Health Care Directive.

The HIPPA Authorization (US only) stands for The Health Information Portability and Accountability Act. It was created in 1996 by the US Congress to protect the privacy of your health information. This law prevents doctors and other medical professionals from discussing your health information with anyone other than your loved one unless they have provided them with a HIPPA release form. This is very important because even you as the caregiver cannot access a loved one's medical records or talk to their doctor until they sign a HIPPA form. You can obtain this form from your loved one's doctor's office.

The next document, the Heath Care Power of Attorney, allows a person to grant legal authority to a trusted relative (i.e. you the caregiver) to make health decisions on their behalf. A person with a heath care POA can determine things like where their loved one can live if their conditions worsens, what they can eat, who bathes them, and what medical care they can receive.

A Living Will and/or Advance Heath Care Directive are also two very important documents your loved one must have. A living will is also known as a heath care declaration. It allows you to state what type of medical treatment your loved one does or does not wish to receive if they are no longer able to make this type of decision on their own due to an illness or incapacity. In other words, it is a document that speaks for your loved one when they are no longer able to do so. A living will outline how your loved one wants their end of life care to be handled. They often time include a Do Not Resuscitate (DNR) order or instructions to not insert feeding tubes of any kind if they become unable to eat on their own.

The Advance Heath Care Directive refers to a single legal document that combines a living will and durable healthcare POA. This document provides you with many more options, including the naming of health care agents. This allows you to make decisions about life-sustaining procedures in the event of a terminal condition, persistent vegetative state, and any end state condition.

Financial documents such as financial POA, trusts, and wills are also important to have on file. Just as the medical documents, the financial documents allow you to make important decisions on your loved one's behalf if needed.

Remember, being organized will reduce stress and help you care for your loved one. It has become a lifesaver for me, simply by just being able to put my hand on documents when I need them at a moment's notice. Most families know and understand why it is important to plan for the future, but when it comes to caring for a loved one, most families do not have a plan until a problem arises. However, I must say that the lack of planning does not mean there is a lack of commitment. It just means you need a plan!

For me, avoiding discussions about the future was simply because I did not want to think about changes in my son's life that may involve him no longer being here. I mean, after all, writing a will or buying a life insurance policy forced me to think about the what if's and what could be. To be quite honest, it was just down right depressing, and something I really hated to face. Even writing this gives me a weird feeling in the pit of my stomach!

Nonetheless, I had to plan for the future, and so will you! Failing to plan for future duties, responsibilities, and circumstances may make a bad situation worse. That is something you do not want on your hands. And the loved one you have protected, but avoided those uncomfortable conversations with, will be the one suffering in the end. With that being said, be sure you put together a caregiving plan with your loved one and other family members to help reduce any problems that may arise in the future.

The most important thing I want you to remember when planning is that conversation about caregiving and a caregiving plan is more than one exchange. It is a give and take type of dialogue. It is a discussion that takes place over time that involves you as the caregiver, the one being cared for, family members, and other important people who will be a part of the planning process. So, remember, it is never too early to start talking and planning.

CHECKLIST

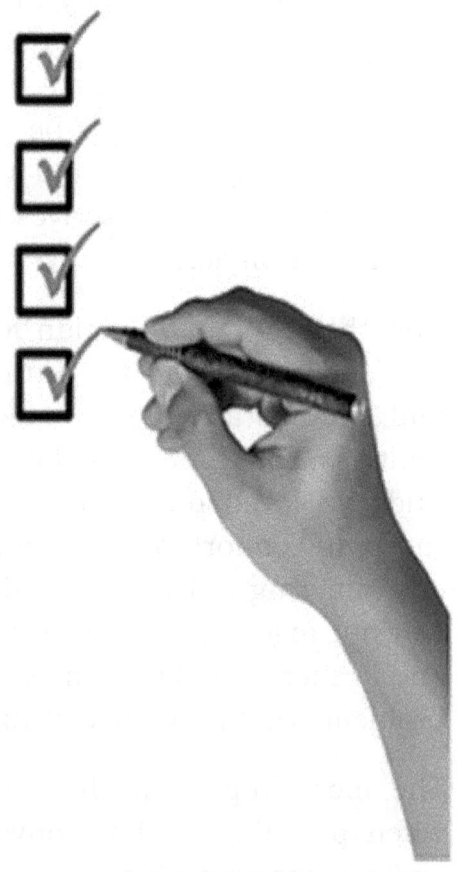

NOTES

Chapter 13
The New Normal

Some of you may ask what I mean by the new normal. Well, I will just say life has never been the same since June 18, 2001. My days have been filled with the hustle and bustle of everything you can possibly think of, and my nights have been filled with thoughts of what ifs, what could be, and what's next. I go to bed with thoughts of the next day's agenda, even though I tell myself each night that I am going to just turn it over to God and allow Him to work it out. Still, I wake up with thoughts of a million and one things that probably have to be altered to that very same agenda.

Feelings of sadness, guilt, worry, anger, and most of all, uncertainty sometime continue to consume me. As the reality of change or disability becomes clearer, indefinite feelings of loss sets in. Even the people closest to me are not always able to see or accept the changes in my son. Why? You ask. Maybe it is because he looks like he always did. I truly believe this is why I do not get the support I really need and why I often feel depressed, isolated, and alone. Yeah, the new normal.... that's it for me. However, even though every day is filled with tons of unexpected curveballs, I try hard to push through and hold my head up as I smile at the world as it sometimes puts a whipping on me— even worse than the ones my grandmother used to give me with her switches. But hey, this is life and as I stated earlier, defining why what happened, happened and keeping my perspective has allowed me to somehow push through.

My son and I both maneuver through various stages of care and adjustment since his brain injury. This is the normal for us, or should I say, the new normal. A caregiver and the survivor will always experience different stages of adjustments; it is simply a part of the journey. The survivor progresses through the critical crisis, intensive care unit, rehabilitation hospital or center, and finally back home. Almost always, rehabilitation will continue even after returning home. After my son was discharged from his inpatient hospital rehabilitation program, I was able to enroll him into an outpatient day treatment rehabilitation program which was six hours a day, five days a week. Although I felt that normalcy may never return, after years passed, we began to enter into our new normal stage of adjustment. What you must never forget is there is no single definition of new normal that fits every family, especially since every tragic event and circumstance is different.

My son's new normal, on the other hand, is a bit different from mine because a brain injury brings on uncertainties like nothing you have ever seen or heard of. His new normal started the day he got diagnosed with a severe traumatic brain injury, not the day of his rehabilitation session, or the day he realized he had to relearn all the basic things one takes for granted, such as feeding, dressing, and bathing himself. His days are filled with moments of highs and lows, ups and downs, laughter and tears... all in the same day. Heck, sometimes all in the same hour. His life has been changed dramatically. He often carries guilt for having this new normal change his life, as well as everyone else's life around him. I am sure he hates those words. Sometimes I wonder just how much he understands about his new normal. He still has not gained insight to the severity of his deficits, so I have to try really hard to talk him through many of the challenges life hurls at him. Questions arise like, "Why can't I drive?", or "Why can't I live on my own?", or sometimes curse words that just come out of nowhere. Do I get angry? No, because I understand the frustration of being trapped in your own mind and simply wanting to live your life. How can I get mad? I would probably curse too if I was in his shoes. To be honest, I have said a few here and there due to my own frustration. I do not think anyone will ever really know and understand what my life is truly like as a caregiver. Learning to adapt to the uncertainties life brings me has definitely become my way of life. Now do not get me wrong, I am not saying life is terrible, but what I am saying is I understand what it means to say when the going gets tough, the tough gets going. Yeah, I even wrote a chapter about that in my book *Affirmations for the Mind, Body & Soul*. Discovering how to awaken your inner strength, the power within your soul, is all about developing and increasing your self-confidence and self-love.

Again, there is no single definition of *"new normal"* that fits every family, since each situation and each family is unique. Feelings of sadness, guilt, worry, anger and uncertainty are all part of a caregiver's responses that may lead to undetermined loss, a complex grieving process. Each family's dynamics are different and therefore require strategies that work just for you. The new normal is reorganizing your daily schedule to accommodate and provide for all concerned—your loved one, the caregiver and members of your immediate family. It is true that life is no longer as it once was for all concerned.

My family's journey toward a new normal, discovering and getting a feel for strategies that help me as a caregiver, and my son as the survivor, identify the symptoms of depression, chronic stress and burnout and how to cope and find treatments are all critical to our survival as a whole. Our daily routine changed and so has our thought process of trying to stuff everything into one day and realizing it is NOT going to happen. This, in itself, gets frustrating which causes me to become overwhelmed. Most times it is the routines we have been accustomed to that make it hard to adjust to that new normal. It is so easy to get comfortable in our routines and become creatures of tradition and customs. This causes us to go into panic mode when something comes along to challenge those daily habits. That laundry you usually do every Wednesday morning may have to wait until the weekend. The midweek cleaning you are doing may have to be put off for just a few more days as well. Stop worrying about it, it is not going away; it will be there when you have time to get to it. The new normal can even affect the times you normally cook dinner... So maybe, just maybe, the time will have to change and be a little later than *normal*.

Merriam-Webster defines normal as "conforming to a type, standard, or regular pattern."[iv] In other words, something that is regular, natural, and staying with the general standard. So, with that being said, the new normal for my son and I is the same because it is what we will now know as normal from now on. There are normal or natural days filled with disagreements followed by cease fires. There are normal or natural office visits, normal or natural testing, normal or natural therapy sessions, and possibly even surgeries. The general standard of neuropsychological testing, MRI's, EEG's, and CT Scans become a regular part of a brain injury survivor's treatment. It is on-going and sometimes feels never-ending.

When I do not try so hard, worry so much, do too much, or try to fix everything at once, I feel more comfortable in my caregiver role. Trying to do the best I can on a daily basis, as opposed to trying to be perfect, makes my job a little less scary. So, now you too must remind yourself not to try so hard or worry so much and try to fix everything at once. When you learn to relax, your new normal will inevitably and certainly become normal.

NOTES

Chapter 14
Practice Gratitude

Gratitude is often defined as a feeling of thankfulness or appreciation for something or someone. I know this is often quite challenging. Yet, the rewards of living life and dealing with the challenges that come along with life appreciatively are overflowing. I learned early on in my caregiving walk, the more I display gratitude the happier I am, and the easier the challenges become. The more I give thanks for all I go through in life things just seem to work out more. Doors just seem to open, and the right people just seem to always be there when I need them.

As you may have recognized from what I just stated above, your attitude greatly determines your mindset. When I changed my attitude and mindset, my language changed and so did my life. Yes, that is right. Our attitude and mindset feed one another, so the more grateful we think we are, the more grateful we will actually be. Remember, your brain will take as "fact" whatever you *believe* to be true. This is why it is imperative to practice gratitude on a daily basis. I am not talking about showing gratitude for something that is unlikely to happen, but a genuine appreciation of the positive aspects of daily life. Practicing gratitude and showing appreciation for the simple things in life we often take for granted is the best advice I can offer as you travel this caregiving journey. It is the fuel that ignites my day. Each day, before I get out of bed, I give thanks and express gratitude for simply being able to open my eyes to see a new day.

Another thing I try to do each day is end my day on a positive note right before going to bed each night. I think of at least one positive thing that happened during my day, and I take a moment to *genuinely* feel gratitude for it. I do not worry about other things that may not have taken place as I may have hoped they would, I simply focus on this one thing, and I thank God for it like never before. If you do this at least once daily, with *genuineness*, you too will begin to recognize more to be thankful for.

I understand that fostering a sense of thankfulness may feel like the last thing you would want to do right now, especially after dealing with the hardships of a challenging day of caregiving, but it is actually more important than ever to do so. Gratitude researcher Robert Emmons, a psychology professor at University of California, Davis, told The Huffington Post, "Gratitude reduces all stress, big and small." You know what? I actually think he is right!

I realized that holding on to guilt and bitterness, made me resentful, angry, hostile and aggravated over and over. Doing so delayed my ability to gain access to gratitude and peacefulness. I learned the way to create a sense of gratitude when valid concerns about my son's and my family's future or well-being continued to haunt me, was to catch myself in a negative thought and redirect it...immediately! Recalling the good things in my life is a way to protect myself against anxiety, even if just for a moment.

Practicing gratitude always help me stay focused on the good things about myself and my loved ones. I know it may not change the current situation at hand, but it helps me to take control and calm my own internal raging sea. Here are simple ways to help you practice gratitude during this unfriendly time and it is important that you do so. The health benefits of the practice are worth the work. Research shows practicing gratitude can help regulate and lower blood pressure, help you sleep better, and most importantly, help you live longer. Below are a few methods to get you there:

1. Appreciate everything – No matter how big or how small, show appreciation for it all.

2. Find gratitude in your challenges – This allows you to gain and maintain perspective as you seek to define why things are happening around you.

3. Practice mindfulness – Being mindful of the good and the bad will help you appreciate everything. It will show you that no matter what occurs, there is indeed a purpose for it happening. Staying mindful of the reasons God has chosen you to be "The One" will allow you to always look

for the good in all you do.

4. Keep a gratitude journal – This will help you to also stay focused on the things that are positive in your life. It will increase your positivity, and help you to naturally become more positive. This will also increase your own self-esteem. Being able to see your accomplishments as you record them allows you to be present with your own achievements.

5. Spend time with loved ones – This will increase family bonds and nurture positive behaviors. This allows you to create family memories you can hold near and dear in your heart. When family ties are strengthened, stronger relationships are developed. This is the best thing that can happen for you as the caregiver as well as for the one you are caring for.

6. Improve your happiness in other areas of your life – Harnessing the power of happiness is the key to your well-being. When you are grateful, you are happy, but being happy also makes you grateful! There are several things you can do to increase your happiness. Participating in activities that make you smile, exercising, singing, soaking in a hot tub, or even simply relaxing in front of the television watching your favorite show are all things that can make you happy, causing your endorphins to flow. This will cause your body to seek the feeling it gets when you are happy. Therefore, the more you are happy the more grateful you will become.

Before I was able to grasp the habit of practicing gratitude, I used to find myself taking for granted so many different things in life. We all do it, you know; the simple things like waking up being able to do for yourself without having to depending on any one to do them for you. I made a vow to myself that no matter what happened or how many challenges I faced on this journey, I would try my very best not complain. Doing so allows me to stay motivated which, in turn, causes me to become more willing to put in the effort and commitment it takes to become more grateful.

I can honestly say that practicing gratitude has helped me to see the importance of living one day at a time. I value that each day is a day in itself with its own challenges and wins. Truly understanding that each day has enough trouble of its own allows me to boldly proclaim "now I get it", and so I merely accept the things I cannot change, and change the things I can. I do this all by simply practicing gratitude!

Caregiver's Monthly Challenge

"The Positivity Jar"

This helps me to practice gratitude! Hope it helps you as well. Write down something that made you **happy** <u>every day</u> for a month, then open the jar and read about all the amazing things that happened during the month! Repeat this exercise every month.

NOTES

Chapter 15
My Name is Victory

Like other caregivers, I believe I am a changed person from who I was years ago, before the term *"traumatic brain injury"* ever entered my vocabulary. Throughout this period, I have learned lessons that, for many, take decades to attain. These are the lessons I wish I had been born with, the lessons that have allowed me to access my most genuine authentic self, and the lessons that have molded and shaped me into who I am today, helping to guide our family out of shock, helplessness and hopelessness, and grief, and back into the sunshine.

Though I tried hard for a long time to make my son and I fit in, I eventually found myself shattered and disappointed by the results. So now fitting in is no longer a meaningful goal. Now, I simply wish to lighten my own path in life, to honor and celebrate the things that feel real and alive within me, myself, and I, and to block out the noise and doubt that threaten to discourage me away from my own truth, value, and substance as I travel this caregiver's journey. The two most important lessons I have learned is that *THIS*

TOO SHALL PASS and *YOU WILL SURVIVE!* I never thought I would survive the indefinite grief of losing my son; well, the one God had initially given to me at birth. In the days after our car accident, I remember thinking that I would never be able to go on if he died. It goes without saying that I am eternally grateful I did not lose him completely. However, there was still a loss. He was alive, but I still felt that he was not quite there most of the time. I felt that I would never see him grow up to be on his own like my family and friends' children probably would be and are. It was a period that threatened to pull me into an ocean of depression at times, but I survived it. Now I see that grief and sadness are a natural part of life. What comforts me, as I observe the world these days through the eyes of a caregiver, are the confirmations I receive daily that people are built to withstand mind-boggling, unimaginable, and inconceivable things. Not only that, but I remind myself daily to never forget that we wrestle not against flesh and blood but against principalities, against powers, against the rulers of the darkness of this world, and against spiritual wickedness in high places.

Anxiety, stress, worry, and obsessive thinking are all consequences of living in a fast paced, mentally overwhelming and overpowering society. Never before have I been more convinced that life is simply supposed to be fun and enjoyable. Yes, there will be inevitable struggles, daily challenges, as well as random tests and trials but giving in to self-doubt and negative thinking is destructive and wasteful. These days, my time is spent speaking positive affirmations and daily declarations as I watch my son continue evolving into the man he is becoming. I finally realized that one day life will, without a doubt, come to an end and therefore, I want to live my life in a way knowing that I am going to my grave empty. I want to take my last breath feeling that mine was a celebration of the world and all it has to offer. I want to know that my journey not just as a caregiver, but as a servant, was one filled with love that was given to others in a way it transformed and impacted their lives immensely. On the other hand, I recognize that the people in my life I care for will not be present forever, so I choose to treasure them and celebrate them now. I choose to make each day with them a day to remember. Are they all filled with joyous laughter and happiness? HECK NO! But I do my best to share with them the things I admire about their personality and character, and to hold the hug for a few seconds longer. I strive to tell jokes and laugh more each day. I realize that this is all I get and so I want to hold on to it for as long as I can.

It is not easy sometimes, but I have to believe that whatever the price is for pursuing the life that best fits your soul is worth the risk. It has been for me. It is worth the scars, the tears, and every lesson I learn along the way. I do not want anyone else's life but my own, and why should I? I am happy that God found me worthy of this call. Everyone cannot be a caregiver, you know? I am blessed to be the one God chose to be the messenger to other caregivers that life can be grand and full of joyous times!

Choosing love over fear and gratitude over sorrow has

been the best decision of my life as a caregiver. To be perfectly honest, I have given into fear more often than I would like to admit in my life, and the result is almost always the same: I go into a shell as I down spiral into a hole of depression, and I numb myself in the process. Hence, when I began to choose love, the opposite happened: I opened myself up to the world and allowed the blessings to pour in. I allow God to speak to me through the many signs and wonders He constantly demonstrates to me. I allow my words to be the driving force that keeps me moving forward as I travel this journey. Choosing love allows helps me to choose gratitude, which in turn, allows me to change the way I look at everything. When I first became a caregiver, I looked at our circumstances, and I felt pitiful. I felt that not only my son's and my lives were over, but no matter who we came in contact with they would not want to deal with us for long. Yes, some have indeed disconnected from us, but I look at it as God's will and that He will replace those who have with others who love unconditionally. That is one thing I can truly say I have a deeper understanding of now as a caregiver, and that is the meaning of unconditional love. Families of brain injury are not unfortunate, tarnished, or damaged goods. We are tough! We are resourceful! We know the importance of not taking people, things, or life for granted. We have the opportunity to create a happier life and reality for ourselves because we have experienced personally the gift of life.

I want you to remember life is good. As caregivers, we are so very alive and full of life. Keep the spirit of your family ignited as you go through each day empowering and inspiring others to keep moving forward, making the impossible possible. Sharing in your loved one's pain does not mean fixing it, making sense of it, or covering it. Dealing with challenges is an unavoidable part of being human, and is always a part of a caregiver's life. Learning to let things be can be a lifetime mission. Some days I do very well, but, my God other days I am so limited that I cannot see the forest for the trees. What I have noticed is that on those days, I just let go and allow myself to accept imperfection. I am at ease with life, and peace flows naturally.

NOTES

Chapter 16
Praising Forward

The word forward means ahead. Never ever forget that it is ok to look ahead. During times when things look like they may not be going well, or during times when you may not be able to see the good in any situation, this is the time you must PRAISE FORWARD! This probably sounds insane to you, but trusts me; I know what I am talking about.

My pastor preached a sermon titled "Praising Forward". He took the text from *Isaiah 54:1-5 (MSG)*, which reads, *"Sing, barren woman, who has never had a baby. Fill the air with song, you who've never experienced childbirth! You're ending up with far more children than all those childbearing women."* God says so! *"Clear lots of ground for your tents! Make your tents large. Spread out! Think big! Use plenty of rope, drive the tent pegs deep. You're going to need lots of elbow room for your growing family. You're going to take over whole nations; you're going to resettle abandoned cities. Don't be afraid - you're not going to be embarrassed. Don't hold back - you're not going to come up short. You'll forget all about the humiliations of your youth, and the indignities of being a widow will fade from memory. For your Maker is your bridegroom, his name, God-of-the-Angel-Armies! Your Redeemer is The Holy of Israel, known as God of the whole earth."*

When I heard this sermon, I immediately knew I had to write about it. I had to, because as a caregiver I know all too well about the benefits of *PRAISING FORWARD*. You see, there is an adventure of praising God in every situation—good situations as well as the not-so-good situations. It is always easy to praise God when things are going great in your life. The challenge is praising God when things are at their worst in your life, when things do not appear to be going as they should. As a caregiver, the many ups and downs I have endured have taught me the importance of *PRAISING FORWARD*. You must remember during your seasons of examining and testing, we complain about everything, we blame others, and get angry. However, what we should be doing is praising God for what He has done and what He is about to do. Do not allow the circumstances of this season to cause you to forget that God is able to do exceedingly and abundantly above all you can ever ask or think according to the power that works in YOU. Listen up loud and clear! *Isaiah 59:1 (MSG)* tells us, *"Look! Listen! God's arm is not amputated—he can still save. God's ears are not stopped up—he can still hear."* God is never searching for a solution, and He is never sitting around saying, "Hmmmm, I didn't see this coming." He never does that, ever. It is impossible to blindside God! We just simply cannot do that. There is nothing He does not already know, or nothing He cannot see or do. What I had to do was stop focusing on my problems, and place my problems in the hands of God so that I can focus on His awesome provisions instead.

Praising God makes me happy by freeing anxiety and tension from my life. It relieves me of stress that is not good for me or my loved one. Praising God not only gives me a testimony, but it confuses the enemy. Praise open doors to solutions I never knew existed. Praising God gives us deliverance and hope, but this is only possible if we believe that God is true to His word. One exciting and distinctive characteristic about God and His word is that they are one and the same. Yes! The Bible tells us in *John 1:1(NIV)* that *"In the beginning was the Word, and the Word was with God, and the Word was God."* Another translation states, *"The Word was first, the Word present to God, God present to the Word."* Therefore, there is no need for uncertainty in the things pertaining to God or what He is able to do because He can do anything but fail!

Once I understood that the challenging situations that accompany my life as a caregiver are not designed to make me happy, I was able to move forward in finding ways to make myself happy by praising Him, in other words by *PRAISING FORWARD*. The challenges and hindrances I face as a caregiver are always designed to frustrate and discourage me, but I...yes, I ultimately decided whether these situations would make or break me. One day I realized I had more power than I actually understood I had. My ability to speak life is what got me through many of the toughest times of my life. So, why had I forgotten about this? I do not know. Maybe it was my attitude during those times of testing that affected the outcome of the things I was dealing with.

The sooner I started thinking positive thoughts, the sooner I was able to move forward. That is why it is not only important to *PRAISE FORWARD*, but is imperative that we do it. Our lives depend on it. Some of you may think otherwise, but keep in mind, great things happen under pressure and frustration. Many precious, rare, unusual, peculiar, one of a kind, gemstones are formed from rocks being exposed to high temperature and pressure over long periods of time. So, do not despair; *PRAISE FORWARD*, and count it all joy when you find yourself in challenging situations! Most caregivers actually do well under pressure, because it is this fighting spirit that makes the next chapter even better, the next testimony even greater, or the next book...a best seller.

As I close, I ask the question: What do you do when caregivers need care given? When we are being challenged, mishandled, judged and talked about, pushed aside, and/or when others just do not understand why we make the decisions pertaining to our love ones that we make, we *PRAISE FORWARD*, and teach the one we are caring for to *PRAISE FORWARD* as well!

We never stop believing that God is who He says He is: God our Jehovah-Jireh, our provider; God our YHWH-Raah, our Shepard; God our El Shaddai, The All Sufficient One; God our YHWH Rapha, our Healer; God our YHWH Niss'i, our Banner; God our YHWH Shalom, our Peace. And, finally, He is our El Olam, the Alpha and the Omega, the beginning and the end! He makes the final decision on our lives and the lives in those we care for, not our circumstances and situations. What more do we need? Nothing, so what are you waiting on? *PRAISE FORWARD!*

NOTES

May God bless you as you continue on your caregiver's journey to success.

"Caregiver's Affirmation"

I AM grateful for my life just the way it is.

I AM grateful for my family and love them just the way they are.

Today I will create my own sunshine.

I AM whole and powerful, perfect, and strong.

I AM open to learning lessons of growth daily.

I AM not perfect and will not try to be.

I WILL speak life into the person I care for daily.

I WILL stay positive even when I don't feel like it.

I WILL accept the person I care for just as they are.

I WILL think positive each and every day.

I WILL smile even on the bad days.

I WILL do the best I can.

I WILL not try to be all things to all people at any given time.

I WILL not be afraid to say NO when I need to.

I WILL not feel guilty to take care of myself.

I WILL be my own best friend and encourage myself daily.

I WILL be the best caregiver I can be.

I CAN, and I WILL because

I AM A CAREGIVER!

NOTE TO SELF

(Begin with I am...)

Scriptures That Speak Life and Keep You Inspired

Colossians 3:23-24 (GNT) *"Whatever you do, work at it with all your heart, as though you were working for the Lord and not for people. Remember that the Lord will give you as a reward what he has kept for his people. For Christ is the real Master you serve."*

Matthew 6:25-27 (GNT) *"This is why I tell you: do not be worried about the food and drink you need in order to stay alive, or about clothes for your body. After all, isn't life worth more than food? And isn't the body worth more than clothes? Look at the birds: they do not plant seeds, gather a harvest and put it in barns; yet your Father in heaven takes care of them! Aren't you worth much more than birds? Can any of you live a bit longer by worrying about it?"*

Proverbs 3:5-6 (GNT) *"Trust in the Lord with all your heart. Never rely on what you think you know. Remember the Lord in everything you do, and he will show you the right way."*

Psalms 118:24 (GNT) *"This is the day of the Lord's victory; let us be happy, let us celebrate!"*

2 Corinthians 12:9 (GNT) "But his answer was: "My grace is all you need, for my power is greatest when you are weak." I am most happy, then, to be proud of my weaknesses, in order to feel the protection of Christ's power over me.

Galatians: 5:22-23 (GNT) "But the Spirit produces love, joy, peace, patience, kindness, goodness, faithfulness, humility, and self-control. There is no law against such things as these."

Ephesians 2:9-10 (NIV) "...not by works, so that no one can boast. For we are God's handiwork, created in Christ Jesus to do good works, which God prepared in advance for us to do."

Isaiah 40:3 (NIV) "...but those who hope in the Lord will renew their strength. They will soar on wings like eagles; they will run and not grow weary, they will walk and not be faint."

Luke 24:36 (NIV) "While they were still talking about this, Jesus himself stood among them and said to them, "Peace be with you."

Philippians 4:19 (NIV) "And my God will meet all your needs according to the riches of his glory in Christ Jesus".

Psalm 46:1 (NIV) "God is our refuge and strength, an ever-present help in trouble."

Isaiah 40:29 (NIV) "He gives strength to the weary and increases the power of the weak."

Colossians 3:1-2 (NIV) "Since, then, you have been

raised with Christ, set your hearts on things above, where Christ is, seated at the right hand of God. Set your minds on things above, not on earthly things."

Proverbs 4:23 (NIV) *"Above all else, guard your heart, for everything you do flows from it."*

Numbers 6:24-26 (GNT) *"May the Lord bless you and take care of you; May the Lord be kind and gracious to you; May the Lord look on you with favor and give you peace."*

"Making the Impossible Possible"
My Loved One Medication List – fill out in pencil.

Medication Record	Today's Date:		Birth Date:	
Name:				
Emergency Contact 1:			Phone:	
Emergency Contact 2:			Phone:	

Name of Medication			
Prescribed			
Over the Counter			
Other			
How medication is administered (pill, capsule, injection, patch, ointment)			
Dosage			
What medication looks like (color, size, etc.)			
What the drug is treating (condition)			
Side effects I've experienced			
When to take medication (time of day)			
What not to do when taking medication			
Name of prescriber (doctor's name)			
Name of pharmacy that filled this prescription			
Date I started on this medication			
Date I stopped taking it			

Things my loved one is allergic to: (Drugs & Other Significant Things)	
Name of Drug	*Reaction I get*

Medications tried that caused problems or didn't work.	
Drug	Problem
1.	
2.	
3.	
4.	
5.	

My Loved One's Medical Team Names and Phone Numbers		
My Primary Care Physician	Name:	
	Phone:	
Neurologist	Name:	
	Phone:	
Specialist 2	Name:	
	Phone:	
Pharmacy	Name:	
	Phone:	

TO DO LIST

TASK TO DO	GOAL TO COMPLETE	TASK TO DO	GOAL TO COMPLETE

NOTES

_____
_____
_____
_____
_____
_____
_____
_____

APPOINTMENT REMINDER

(Fill out in pencil)

Here is your friendly reminder that you have an appointment on:

_____ / _____

Month   Day

_____

Time

ABOUT THE AUTHOR

Twylia Reid is a native of Mississippi who currently resides in Savannah, GA with her husband Dexter, and son Mylon. They're a blended family of 4 adult children and 5 grandchildren. She obtained a B.S. Degree in Business Administration at Trident University International, and is a 20-year US Army retiree.

Amazon #1 Best Selling Author, 2018 Congressional Black Caucus Featured Author, 2018 Winner of The Authors Show Top Female Non-Fiction Author, 2017 American Book Fest Best Book Awards Finalist, The Huffington Post Expert Feature Series *"Who's Who – 10 Black Female Experts to Watch in 2018"* selectee, 2017 Indie Author Legacy Award Author of the Year finalist, 2018 AAALAC International Recognized Author, and 2018 ACHI Magazine Author of the Year & Woman of Inspiration Finalist.

Reid is the President/CEO of **Broken Wings**, Inc., a 501(c) 3 non-profit organization designed to provide awareness about traumatic brain injury. She's a speaker, minister, and founder of **Broken Wings Brain Injury Empowerment Group**, an online brain injury support group. Last but not least, she's the founder, and host of Blog Talk Radio's **Conquerors Café** Show.

RECOMMENDED READINGS

Reid, Twylia G. **Broken Wings.** *The journey from tragedy to triumph through my son's traumatic brain injury.* Savannah, Georgia: Broken Wings, 2017.

Reid, Twylia G. **Affirmations For the Mind, Body & Soul:** *A Guide for Survivors of Traumatic Events.* Savannah, Georgia: Broken Wings, 2018.

Additional books by Author Twylia G. Reid:

Reid, Twylia G. **MY JOURNEY GOAL SETTING JOURNAL** Savannah, Georgia: Savannah, Georgia: Broken Wings, 2018.

Reid, Twylia G. **The WORD The Truth & The Light: BIBLE STUDY NOTEBOOK.** Savannah, Georgia: Broken Wings, 2018.

Reid, Twylia G. **A Survivor's Goal Planning Journal** *A Brain Injury Survivor's Guide to Goal Setting.* Savannah, Georgia: Broken Wings, 2018.

Reid, Twylia G. **PRAY BELIEVE RECEIVE Prayer Journal**. Savannah, Georgia: Broken Wings, 2018.

For book signing and speaking requests:

Email: info@twyliareid.com

Websites:
www.twyliareid.com
www.brokenwingsinc.org
www.conquerorscafe.com

Facebook:
www.facebook.com/authortwyliareid
www.facebook.com.BWINC
www.facebook.com/conquerorscafe

Linked In: www.linkedin.com/in/twyliareid
Twitter: www.twitter.com/tgreid02
Instagram: www.instagram.com/twyliareid02

References

---

[i] The National Institute of Mental Health. *Depression.* Accessed 30 Sept. 2018. https://www.nimh.nih.gov/health/topics/depression/index.shtml.

[ii] Fight or flight response. *Wikipedia.com*, Wikipedia, Accessed 30 Sept. 2018. https://en.wikipedia.org/wiki/Fight-or-flight_response.

[iii] "Conqueror." *Merriam-Webster.com*, Merriam-Webster, Accessed 30 Sept. 2018. www.merriam-webster.com/dictionary/conqueror.

[iv] "Normal." *Merriam-Webster.com*, Merriam-Webster, Accessed 03 Oct. 2018. https://www.merriam-webster.com/dictionary/normal.

www.ingramcontent.com/pod-product-compliance
Lightning Source LLC
Chambersburg PA
CBHW051944160426
43198CB00013B/2300